Storyteller, writer, poet, musician[...]d
folklore, Stuart McHardy is stee[...].
Since graduating with a history [...]e
1970s he has found ongoing in[...],
surviving story and music traditions. His research has led him far
beyond Scotland and he has lectured and performed in many different
parts of the world. Whether telling stories to children gathered round him
in a circle or lecturing to adults at Edinburgh University's Office of Lifelong
Learning on such topics as the Picts or the Jacobites, Stuart's enthusiasm
and love of his material make him an entertaining and stimulating
speaker. His wide ranging interests and talents have led to him lecturing,
telling stories and sometimes singing in various museums, visitor centres
and other venues in a truly inimitable fashion.

His own enthusiasm and commitment have led to him re-interpreting
much of the early history, mythology and legends of Early Western Europe.
Combining the roles of scholar and performer gives McHardy an unusually
clear insight into tradition and he sees connections and continuities that
others may have missed. As happy singing an old ballad as analysing
ancient legends he has held such diverse positions as Director of the Scots
Language Resource Centre and President of the Pictish Arts Society. He
lives in Edinburgh with the lovely Sandra and they have one son, Roderick.

www.wittins.demon.co.uk

By the same author:

The Quest for Arthur
The Quest for the Nine Maidens
On the Trail of Scotland's Myths & Legends
Tales of the Picts
Strange Secrets of Ancient Scotland
Scots Poems to be read aloud
Tales of Whisky and Smuggling

Now available in Luath's *On the Trail of* series

On the Trail of the Holy Grail

STUART McHARDY

Luath Press Limited

EDINBURGH

www.luath.co.uk

First Published 2006

The paper used in this book is recyclable.
It is made from low chlorine pulps produced in a low energy,
low emission manner from renewable forests.

Printed and bound by
Bookmarque Ltd., Croydon

Maps by Jim Lewis

Typeset in 10.5 point Sabon

Contents

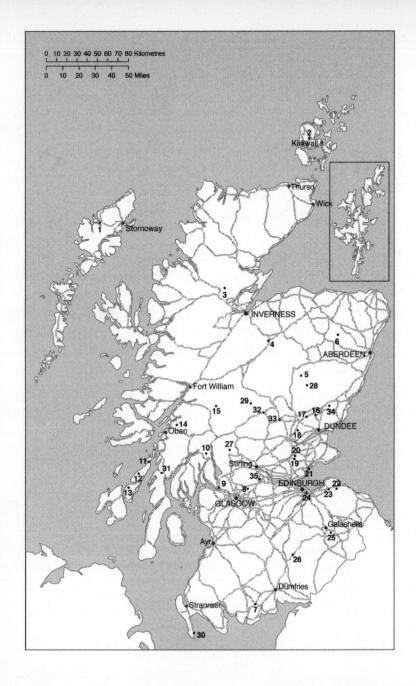

Key to Map

Chronology

7th century	expansion of Northumbria
664	Synod of Whitby
685	Picts defeat Northumbrians at Dunnichen
704	death of Adomnan biographer of Columba
717	Columban Church expelled from land of the Picts
793	start of Viking raids
815	Battle of Athelstaneford of which Northumbrians defeated by Picts and Scots
847	Kenneth Macalpin King of Picts and Scots
900	Scotland annexes Strathclyde
1005	birth of Macbeth, Mormaor of Moray
1057	Macbeth killed by Malcolm III
1066	Normans conquer England
1140	Geoffrey of Monmouth's *History of the Kings of Britain*
c. 1180	Wolfram von Eschenbach's *Parzifal*
1190	Chretien de Troyes' *Perceval*
1190	First Crusade
c. 1200	Robert de Boron writes *The Chronicle of the History of the Grail*
1204	*The Chronicle of Helinandus*
1225-1237	*The Vulgate Cycle*
1307	Templars purged
1309	Trial of Templars in Scotland
1446	Rosslyn Chapel founded by Sir Wlliam St Clair
1485	printing of Malory's *Morte D'Arthur*

1859	Tennyson starts writing Arthurian poems
1889	Mark Twain writes *A Yankee at the Court of King Arthur*
1975	*Monty Python and the Holy Grail* film
1982	Publication of *Holy Blood, Holy Grail*
2003	Publication of *The Quest for the Nine Maidens*
2004	Publication of *The Da Vinci Code*

Preface

IN THE FILM *Monty Python and the Holy Grail* there is a scene in which Arthur (Graham Chapman) fights the Black Knight (John Cleese). Even after having both arms and legs chopped off, the Black Knight calls Arthur a coward for refusing to carry on fighting. This is a satire on the idea of the chivalrous and fearless knight, a concept which was central to the widespread popularity of the stories of King Arthur and the Round Table. This vision of King Arthur and the Knights of the Round Table, which the Python team were satirising and can perhaps be seen at its most fanciful in Hollywood films like *A Yankee at the Court of King Arthur* and the musical *Camelot*, is an example of how the story of Arthur has taken hold of the public imagination since Geoffrey of Monmouth first wrote about him hundreds of years ago. As I write this, a court case has just finished in London. Michael Baigent and Richard Leigh, the authors of *Holy Blood, Holy Grail*, unsuccessfully sued Dan Brown, author of the immensely popular *The Da Vinci Code*, for stealing their ideas. Both books stem from the fascination that the idea of the Holy Grail has held over the public imagination for most of the last millennium. The Grail has come to symbolise many things, the search for ancient knowledge, the discovery of arcane treasure, and the quest for personal enlightenment. In Baigent and Leigh's version of the story, the idea of the Grail is presented as a cover for the 'reality' that Jesus Christ survived crucifixion, married Mary Magdalene, and had children whose descendants still walk the earth today. This is predicated on the notion that the *San Greal* or Holy Dish really means *Sang Real*, Holy Blood. In Walter W. Skeat's *The Concise Etymological English Dictionary of the English Language*, we find the following: 'Its etymology was changed from *San Greal* (Holy Dish) to *Sang Real*, that is Royal Blood, perversely taken to mean "Real Blood"'. A more problematic point is that if Jesus did survive hanging on the cross, how can he be the Son of God who was dead and rose again? If he was just a man, what is particularly significant about his descendants?

The Holy Grail itself has been subjected to a great deal of investigation and speculation and has inspired writers and artists consistently for nearly a thousand years. As a basis for creative inspiration it is just one of the themes linked to what is generally known as The Matter of Britain. This is the collection of stories about 'King' Arthur and his knights that were developed into glorious feudal Romances but appear originally to have been truly ancient oral traditions amongst the Celtic-speaking tribes of Britain in the 1st Millennium. The Holy Grail combines themes and characters from The Matter of Britain with themes and characters – from what can only be described as Christian mystic tradition – to create a concept that today has as powerful a hold on the public imagination as it did when the idea first appeared in Britain in the closing years of the 12th century. And nowadays the Grail is known all over the world. In this book I hope to show that behind the myths and legends that are the cultural legacy of the indigenous peoples of Britain there lies an awesome reality that still exists in the landscape, or seascape, today. And that physical reality is in Scotland.

CHAPTER ONE

An Opening Door

*The Grail in literature – Pagan and Christian roots – Crusades
– 'King' Arthur – oral traditions – growth of Romances –
roots among Celtic-speaking peoples – links to Germanic
mythology – situation in Scotland*

THE CONCEPT OF THE Holy Grail as we now know it is essentially a
literary one. The idea of the Grail as sacred goblet first occurs in
Chrétien de Troyes' *Perceval*, an unfinished poem written in late
twelfth-century France. We know little of the author other than
that he was associated with the court of Marie, Countess of
Champagne in the late 12th century, and is thought to have spent
some time at the court of Philip, Count of Flanders before the
count went off on Crusade in 1191. While at this time literacy
was no longer the absolute prerogative of the Church, it seems
likely that Chrétien, like Geoffrey of Monmouth – who had written about King Arthur in England half a century earlier – was a
member of the clergy. *Perceval* is clearly inspired by the corpus of
Arthurian tales that Geoffrey of Monmouth had already made
popular throughout much of Europe. That these tales were originally part of the oral traditions of the indigenous peoples of
Britain is undeniable. In Chrétien's story of the knight Perceval,
the hero comes to the court of the mysterious Fisher King while
a young maiden carries the Grail itself in a procession. It is
described as being made of gold and set with precious stones.
While this tale drew on much older traditions, particularly, as we
shall see, in the Welsh story of Peredur, it began a process where
the Grail has been seen as the ultimate object of chivalric quest.

The specific idea of the Grail as a cup or chalice was a slightly later development first occurring in Robert de Boron's *Joseph d'Aramithie* written around 1200.

The Grail draws upon both pagan and Christian roots and in twelfth-century France Chrétien used it as a motif for writing about armour-clad knights and fair ladies in a way that set the style for centuries to come. The Round Table itself first occurs in *Roman de Brut* written by the Norman poet Wace in 1155, who drew on the Breton storytelling tradition. The world of handsome aristocratic knights with their attendant squires, great warhorses, and full-body armour is one that has continued to inspire writers and artists. This chivalrous world bears no resemblance at all to the reality of the world in which the original Arthur flourished, and from which the oldest ideas underpinning the notion of the Holy Grail themselves emerged. It was a world, however, that found a ready audience and *Perceval* was only the first of a whole series of Romances that spread the idea of the Holy Grail throughout Europe from the 12th century onwards, initially against the background of the Crusades.

The Crusades, which took place over the next two hundred years, were ongoing attempts to wrest control of Jerusalem back from Muslim hands and were particularly brutal, though individual acts of bravery and honourable behaviour did occur. The motivation for the Crusades, though in many cases seen as an opportunity for both glory and plunder, were generally presented as essentially religiously-driven. What greater sign of devotion could a king, a noble or a knight show than laying his life on the line to try and take the most sacred city of the Christians from the control of the infidel Saracens? The fact that Jerusalem was also sacred to the Muslim Saracens and the Jews scattered throughout Europe, Africa and Asia was of no consequence. At this time we can see that the concept of chivalry and honour in battle was closely bound up with this notion of fighting for Christ. The actuality of honour in battle, however, pre-dates the Middle Ages by a long time and had been an integral part of tribal warrior society throughout much of Eurasia. Whatever the actuality of the situation, the idea of Christian service became intimately involved with the idea of the search for the Holy Grail.

The idea of honour in battle was intrinsic to the traditions of the British tribal warrior societies where the Arthurian tales first occurred, and the idea of the 'square go', where combatants from different groups fight one on one, is something that is attested in many societies, perhaps the best known example being the battle between David and Goliath, each chosen as the champion of their people. The ideas which underpin the Arthurian stories and the idea of the Grail survive precisely because they are rooted in human behaviour and belief. The idea of the quest itself, whether for the Grail, for personal enlightenment, religious initiation or knowledge of one kind or another is common to all humanity. The Crusades were themselves a personal quest for many of those who took part in them and particularly in Scotland the idea of the Grail quest has become confused because of associations with men to whom the Crusades were of fundamental importance, the Knights Templar, a point to which we will return.

Geoffrey of Monmouth writing in England half a century earlier had undoubtedly influenced Chrétien. Both were drawing on an extant body of stories that were part of the common cultural inheritance of people throughout Europe, an inheritance that crossed both national and linguistic boundaries. It was Geoffrey who popularised the figures of Arthur, Merlin, Lancelot, Galahad and others to the French speaking Anglo-Norman audiences of his time. His writing was based to a considerable extent on traditional tales and legends and he claimed to have had access to an ancient book which gave him the material for his *Life of Merlin* and *History of the Kings of Britain*. Although stimulated by these ancient tales, the authors of the Romances drew upon notions of chivalry and courtesy which fascinated their aristocratic audiences. Chivalry was an abstraction of the requirements of knighthood in the feudal society of the time, which apart from the obligations of service and loyalty, aspired to the notion of fair play, even towards enemies and the poor or oppressed. Another essential element of the chivalrous knight was being ever ready to help members of the female sex, particularly widows, of whom there were many created as a result of the Crusades. In reality such attitudes would appear to have been reserved for those the knights considered their social equals. Likewise the notion of courtesy required the knight to be humble and modest as well as honest and generous. The historical records of the period show ideals to have been precisely that, ideals. It is not difficult to see the attraction of the Arthurian knights like Lancelot and Gawain, who were virtuous, courageous and paragons of virtue, even if ultimately flawed.

Like Geoffrey, Chrétien was adapting material that had long been part of popular culture. The Matter of Britain as Arthurian tales became known, was already a recurring theme in the Breton Lays as well as surviving in all the areas where P-Celtic dialects had been spoken, even those like Scotland and England where Germanic language forms had become dominant. P-Celtic is the name given to the languages that survive as Welsh, Breton and the revived Cornish. It included the Pictish language that disappeared with other northern British dialects around a thousand years ago. P-Celtic is so called in contrast with Q-Celtic which survives in modern Irish, Scottish Gaelic and the revived Manx tongue. Gaelic *ceann* meaning head occurs in Welsh as *pen*, *mac* for son of, as *map*. This is not the only difference but the one chosen by linguists to differentiate between the languages that are believed to have started out as dialects of the same tongue, with Q-Celtic thought to be the older form. In 1st Millennium Britain both language groups were spoken over much of the British Isles.

Stories that have appeal to widespread audiences have always survived language change, and it would appear that too much emphasis has been placed on language as a means of understanding our past, particularly in Britain. In England the Arthurian tales, in French, were popular amongst the Anglo-Norman community and were often presented by travelling troubadours often in the form of songs accompanied by playing the harp, and preceded by a story of what the song was about. Although such presentations were increasingly taking place in the stone built castles of the nobles they were a development of the storytelling traditions common to all the peoples of northern Europe. These had arisen over millennia amongst the early European tribal peoples and in fact the storytelling tradition survives today. Although currently undergoing a revival in many parts of the world, storytelling did not die out as a result of either spreading literacy or the eventual development of mass produced books through the use of the printing press. One of the very first great popular works of mass-produced publishing in Britain, an early best-seller, was Thomas Malory's *Morte D'Arthur* in the latter years of the 15th century showing that the popularity of the Matter of Britain had retained its popularity since the time of Geoffrey of Monmouth. Alongside the literary works people were continuing to tell the traditional stories at a local level. It is one of the aspects of the tenacity of the storytelling tradition that as long as there is an audience the stories will live on. Even today with films, DVDs and television there are people who 'have the gift of the gab' who tell stories informally in pubs and other social situations, generally without thinking of themselves as storytellers. We all know one or two such people.

While we can see how Geoffrey, Chrétien and the other

Romance writers developed their material for their aristocratic audience, an example of the continuity with the far past is obvious in their use of names copied or developed from characters originating in the original versions of the tales. However far the stories had developed from their ancient originals, and some of Geoffrey's historical episodes are fictional to the point of fantasy, they were still rooted in ancient reality. Even today the figure of King Arthur and his fictional feudal court holds its appeal. The original Arthur was not a king, but Geoffrey, Chrétien de Troyes and these who followed them wrote for an audience for whom the ideal of the king had superseded earlier models of the hero.

Camelot, as portrayed in the Hollywood film of the same name many centuries later, is a case in point. Here the natural order is presented as being the king at the top, his noble aristocrats around him and the rest of the poor benighted human race having no more function than to keep these self-regarding aristocrats in luxury. The men are all handsome and strong, the women beautiful and virtuous. This of course tends also to be the case in some of the most popular tales within the oral tradition, though reality is always ready to intrude. Such oral traditions had moral and educational requirements within the relatively closed communities in which they were originally told. However the stories developed by Chrétien, Geoffrey and the rest were created primarily for entertainment, rather than edification and in the realms of fiction there are few rules. And though the idea of the Holy Grail was rooted in ancient tradition it was developed at a time when the reality of the Crusades had a major impact on all levels of society, particularly amongst those most likely to read the Romances, or have them read aloud. In fact Chrétien's motif fell like a ripe seed into fertile soil and once he had written *Perceval* there was a burst of writing on the topic that created a whole series of works that ensured the Matter of Britain became, and stayed, part of the cultural inheritance of all of Western Europe. The idea of the Grail quest implicitly linked the idea of the chivalrous knight and his quest for enlightenment to the quest to free Jerusalem from the infidel.

Chrétien wrote *Perceval* in the 1180s and this was followed by what are known as the *First* and *Second Continuations* over the next two decades. It is unclear who wrote these two works but the authors were drinking from the same well as Chrétien. By the time of the *Second Continuation* other writers had begun producing similar work. Robert de Boron wrote *The Romance of the History of the Grail, Joseph of Arimathea, Merlin* and his own version of *Perceval* in the first decade of the 13th century. An anonymous work the *High Book of the Grail* had also appeared by 1210. A further series of works followed, which we now know as the Vulgate Cycle, a series of four works entitled *Lancelot, Quest of the Holy Grail, History of the Holy Grail* and *Romance of the Grail*, all written by 1250. The idea of the Grail had clearly taken a firm grip on both the imagination of writers and the interest of their audience. Also in this period Manessier wrote a *Third Continuation* of Chrétien's *Perceval* and this was followed by a *Fourth* written by Gerbert de Montreuil. The popularity of this material was not limited to France and England where the Norman aristocracy were dominant. The German writers Wolfram von Eschenbach with his *Parzival* and Heinrich von dem Turlin with *The Crown* reflect the widespread audience for books on the topic. All of these books drew to great or lesser extent on the French traditions of the Geste and Chanson, the tales and ballads of the travelling storytellers and musicians who toured the castellated homes of the nobles of north-western Europe in the period. These professional entertainers can be seen as the natural successors to the bards who told and re-told the ancient stories of the earlier tribal peoples of Britain, some of whom were also itinerant. To think of the bards within the Celtic-speaking people as something unique however would be a mistake. The storytelling tradition is common to all humanity and while much had been made of the love of poetry amongst the early Irish and Welsh peoples which gave rise to so many surviving stories, the same was just as true of their neighbours, whether over the English Channel in Brittany or over the North Sea in Scandinavia. The Viking poetic and story-telling tradition has in fact had a great effect on how traditional material has developed throughout the British Isles, something that is too often ignored. It is no doubt partially due to the ongoing and widespread popularity of Arthurian stories that too much attention has been focused on what is presented as Celtic tradition and the interlinking of thematic material with the parallel traditions amongst the Germanic-speaking peoples has been relatively ignored. At a truly fundamental level they have much in common, and in fact would appear to come from essentially common roots.

Scholars have long accepted that some of the 'Celtic' roots of the Grail can be found in *The Mabinogion*, the great collection of early Welsh traditional material. And some have seen these tales as having been heavily influenced from Ireland, which after all is but a short boat journey from north Wales. It is one of the anomalies of so-called Celtic scholarship that throughout the 20th-century book after book purporting to analyse the cultural inheritance of the early warrior societies of the Celtic-speaking peoples managed to ignore the longest lasting such society. In Scotland the Q-Celtic speaking, tribal, warrior society of the Highland Gael did not die out until the middle of the 18th century and as we shall see it is in what we now call Scotland that the original pagan source of what in time became the Holy Grail can be found today. The clan society of Highland Scotland that survived until the years following the brutal battle of Culloden in 1746 was still essentially a Celtic-speaking Iron Age tribal warrior society, with all of the social, political and cultural baggage that entailed. It was still extant long after similar societies had disappeared in the rest of the British Isles and most of Europe. Far too much emphasis has been put on Irish influence on Scottish history and culture though there are obvious shared themes and concepts with both Irish and Welsh material. Some such traditions can also be seen as having a great deal in common with Norse traditions. The situation is that in both Ireland and Wales many of the great stories arising from the ancient traditions of the indigenous people were written down a thousand years ago. In Scotland if we ever had similar versions of our traditional material in written form, they were destroyed in a series of invasions by our Southern neighbours, as well as the Vikings, and in the fanatical vandalism that was part of the Scottish Protestant Reformation in the 16th century. The Protestant reformers vandalised monasteries throughout Scotland and it was in monasteries that early records were always kept. Stories however, continued to be told here, not only amongst the clanspeople, but it is in surviving tales from amongst the last warrior society in Britain that we will find the key to the origin of the Grail itself.

The obsession with using language as a defining aspect of historical analysis has led to many misunderstandings. Languages change continually and to try to define people either ethnically or historically by how they speak is silly. In this respect we must reconsider the very idea of 'Celtic'. Much has been made in the past half century of the idea of pan-Celticism. Briefly put this suggests that there is a cultural and historical unity underlying all those areas where Celtic languages were, or still are spoken. This encompasses most of the British Isles and Brittany. In fact the very idea of Celtic peoples is very recent, as was pointed out by Professor Simon James in his book *The Atlantic Celts*. He points out that the term Celtic in its modern sense arose in the 18th century, originally as a term to describe the language group that encompassed the Irish, Scots, Welsh, Manx. Cornish and Breton tongues. This in itself arose from the analysis of languages that developed into the theoretical notion of the Indo-European language family. Essentially the theory states that most languages over the area from Western Europe to the Indian sub-continent are descended from a common root. This concept was involved with a corresponding idea that most of that vast area was 'civilised' or at least conquered, by advanced warrior societies coming out from the central Eurasian plain at some point in the distant past. That is not an idea that holds much water today. There was no way that a member of any of the 'Celtic' language groups before the 18th century would have ever referred to themselves as Celtic; they would not have even known what it meant. Between the usage of the ancient Greek term Keltoi, which appears to have meant no more than 'northerners' and the development of the Indo-European language theory, the term had been used, extremely rarely, as a botanic description.

In fact, the so-called ancient Celtic societies of Ireland and Scotland were interpenetrated and sometimes overlaid in the latter part of the 1st Millennium, by incoming settlements of Scand-ina-vian peoples who spoke Northern Germanic languages. This was before the old stories were written down. Later we shall look at the reality that these incoming settlers, who followed after the raiding Vikings, came from a part of the world with which the peoples of Britain had been in regular contact for thousands of years before the Romans even set foot on these islands.

Today many people look to the past to try and make sense of what increasingly seems a dark future in a present where govern-ments and corporations work together on an agenda that is to say the least problematic. In this light, the attraction of the Holy Grail as a representation of all that is noble and aspiring within the human spirit is understandable. We always need hope, and many people reject the safe platitudes and hierarchic organisation of organised religions. Others turn to those religions to find succour in a time of need, which can make them susceptible to the machinations of political and religious leaders whose primary concern is the advancement of their own power. In some ways perhaps the symbol of the Holy Grail can be seen as a counter to this specifically masculine behaviour and it has been seen by many as an essentially feminine symbol – a symbol, of hope, regeneration and rebirth. As we shall see the physical origin of the ideas that gave rise to the Grail is something that has long been associated with such ideas.

CHAPTER TWO

The Warrior Way

Arthur – Gododdin – warrior society – tribal system –
kinship not kingship – cattle-raiding – Scots not Irish –
language situation – cultural commonalties –
Geoffrey of Monmouth – Nine Maidens sites –
Scotland outside the Roman world

BEFORE WE GO ANY further, we must look closer at the Arthurian background of the Holy Grail. The figure of King Arthur with his chivalric Knights of the Round Table has become one of the whole world's great literary and artistic motifs. Ever since Geoffrey of Monmouth introduced King Arthur in the middle of the 12th century, there has been a regular resurgence of interest in this heroic figure. However the general view of him by the 20th century, as a noble and virtuous Christian king ruling over a feudal type society is a long way from the original Arthur. The earliest known literary mention of Arthur is in a poem called The Gododdin, written in Archaic North Brythonic a P-Celtic tongue, composed around the year 600, in or near Edinburgh. The reference to Arthur is significant as it occurs in the description of one of the sixty warriors described in the poem, one Gwallawg who 'although he fed the ravens, was no Arthur.' This apparently cryptic comment tells us a lot. The reference to feeding the ravens is a common motif from all of the early traditions of north-western Europe, being as common in Norse tradition as in those of Ireland, Wales and of course Scotland. The reference is to the reality that ravens, crows or corbies, would descend on battlefields to pick at the corpses of the fallen, usually starting with the eyes. We can go further and say that the raven in this context was also seen as a symbol of Goddesses like the Morrigan in Irish tradition who haunted battlefields in the shape of a crow and there are other mentions of maidens who turn into ravens to attack some of Arthur's knights.[1] The idea of warrior maidens – Peredur actually fights with a group of armed witches significantly nine in number – occurs across north-western Europe, the best known Norse (Germanic) ones being the Valkyrie, handmaidens to the God Odin, who also sometimes occur as a group of nine. Their primary function was to select dead warriors from the battlefield to enter Valhalla, the warrior heaven of Norse mythology. Like much early tradition, such poetic imagery draws on what were actual realities in the lives of its audience. It is worth remembering that poetry was considered a high art amongst all the warrior peoples of Europe and that most poets or bards were, like Aneurin who composed the Gododdin, warriors themselves. He was in the battle himself and appears to have been the sole survivor of the battle.

The reference to Arthur in this context tells us something specific. The way Aneurin refers to Arthur, makes it quite clear that his audience were well aware of who he was talking about. This reference suggests that Arthur was a by-word for martial prowess, a great warrior, even an exemplary one. The possibility therefore exists that there was already a mythic warrior or hero called Arthur, on whom the supposedly historical Arthur of the 6th century might well have modelled himself. However good a combatant Gwallawg was, he was not as good as Arthur. We should note that the reference is to Arthur, not King Arthur, or Prince Arthur or even Arthur the Chief. At this period the use of the term king is itself anachronistic because amongst the Celtic-speaking tribal warrior peoples of 6th and 7th century Britain there is no evidence that there were kings. The term or something like it, 'cynyng', was in use amongst the Anglian Northumbrians who at this period were beginning to expand and develop into what we would nowadays accept as a something like a nation state. It was their expansion that probably forced the surrounding tribes to become more centralised and their military endeavours more structured. This in time gave rise to the role of the king though at this stage it would appear that society in Scotland was still essentially tribal. The various Arthurian stories and tales that have survived subsequent to *The Gododdin* do so in versions that were written down considerably later and almost always by monks, who were educated in the Bible and Classical Greek and Latin scholarship and thus were well used to the idea of kings. This is true of the earliest annals and other documentation from Britain. The Romans who earlier described these peoples made it clear that the peoples whom they were fighting were tribal, and did not have a hierarchy either like their own or in any way akin to the later feudal system that underpins the stories as told by Geoffrey of Monmouth, Chrétien de Troyes and the other Romancers. One of these Roman commentators, Dio Cassio actually refers to the tribes of northern Britain as being democratic.

The name Gododdin, which is what this P-Celtic speaking tribal people appear to have called themselves, is generally accepted to be the same as the term Votadini, used by the Romans to describe the tribal people who lived in south-east Scotland a few centuries before the poem was composed. John T Koch makes the point that until recently most interpretations of the Gododdin have presented the raid described as having been organised by one *Myndyyg Mynfavwr*, a king probably living on Dyn Eidyn, now Edinburgh Castle Rock.[2] Koch tells us that the phrase '*mnydyyg mynfavwr*' in fact means the 'court on the hill' or something close to it and does not refer to a person at all. It is also notable that in the sixty descriptions of warriors that make up the Gododdin there is no mention of rank, each of the warriors is presented as being pretty much the same as the next. This speaks of the realities of tribal warrior society where we know that war-bands were led by the best warrior available and not necessarily the chief of the tribe or clan. Given that tribes are essentially defined by being formed of people from the same kin-group, i.e. they are all blood relations; it is not difficult to understand how such warriors would all know who was best fitted to lead them. This is not to say that there were no gradations in society, simply that in a raiding band from a restricted kin-group, it would make sense for the warriors to choose their best warrior or strategist to lead. When the smaller war-bands merged to form larger groupings, as we know happened spectacularly in instances like the so-called Barbarian Conspiracy between Picts, Scots and Saxons that overwhelmed Hadrian's Wall in 360 AD, there were no doubt complicated negotiations necessary to choose who was to lead. It is perhaps also instructive to compare what happened at the only reported major battle between the Romans and the Caledonians in AD 80, *Mons Graupius*. There the Caledonians are said to have been led by one Calgacus, whose name has been translated as The Swordsman, a good name for a warrior, and Tacitus, who reported the battle, makes no mention of him as having any specific rank.

This practice of having a specialist to lead the raiding band was still extant into the 18th century amongst the Highland clans of the Scottish Highlands, the descendants of tribal warrior societies of the sixth and seventh centuries. It is also true that the Highland clans were known for being 'addicted to raiding', a phrase first used of warriors in the north Britain by Dio Cassio, writing at the beginning of the 3rd century. Raiding other tribes or clans, generally to steal cattle, the main measure of moveable wealth in all early pastoral societies, was part of ancient Eurasian society as a whole, although it lasted almost into modern times in Scotland. As Carlo Ginzberg wrote in *Ecstasies*:

In the legendary biography of the young hero, the theft of live-
stock carried out in league with their contemporaries was an
obligatory stage, virtually an initiation ritual. It respected a very
ancient mythical model, amply documented in the Indo-
European cultural milieu.[3]

The battle that forms the action of the Gododdin has been presented as being some sort of dynastic struggle, but given the type
of society its warriors were part of, it appears at least as likely to
have been a raid. Raiding was after all what warriors did. It is
also worth considering whether the location of the actual battle,
Catraeth was in the area now known as Raith, in Fife, rather than
Catterick in far-off Yorkshire. If it was a cattle-raid gone wrong –
and there are plenty instances of this happening in Scottish history
– it would be a devastating event within the tribal community that
sent out the raiders, and of much more significance to the poet
telling the story than the actions of some supposed king. That
such raiding was a central function of the tribal warrior society
over another millennium in Scotland is shown by the similarities
between the Roman references and the propaganda put out by the
British Government after the Battle of Culloden in 1746 where the
glens of Highland Scotland were almost all garrisoned by troops
supposedly to counter cattle theft. I have written of this elsewhere
but it is also perhaps pertinent that a Pictish Symbol Stone from
Dull in Perthshire shows a group of warriors who appear to be
setting out on a raid.[4] Some are on horseback, others on foot and
accompanied by dogs, most likely trained to work silently herding
cattle alongside them. There are hundreds of these symbol stones
in Scotland attributed to the Picts, the group of tribal peoples that
the Romans encountered and the stones are generally thought to
have been sculpted between the 6th and 9th centuries, though some
people think their origins may be considerably earlier.

According to the Romans the Picts, sometimes also referred

to as Caledonians, were the people who inhabited Britain north of Hadrian's Wall and thus incorporated tribes such as the Gododdin, or Votadini who were P-Celtic speaking and the Scots of Dalriada, in modern Argyll, who spoke a form of Q-Celtic. The long established belief that the Scots came into Argyll from Ireland around 500 AD has been shown to be based on nothing more than an early medieval document written more than half a millennium after the event and with no archaeological, linguistic or other evidence to back it up.[5] We shall be returning to Argyll and the capital of the Scots at Dunadd in Kilmartin.

The reason that the earliest reference to Arthur originated in Scotland was simply the fact that a considerable number, probably the majority of the peoples of southern and eastern Scotland in the 7th century, spoke the language now described as Archaic North Brythonic which was effectively one of the ancestors of modern Welsh. The Gododdin, inhabiting the Lothians and perhaps at one point spreading as far south as Bamburgh, the Britons of Strathclyde whose area stretched from Dumbarton on the Clyde to Carlisle and the people who formed the later kingdom of the Picts north of the Forth-Clyde line, all spoke forms of this language. While it is possible, even likely that there were small numbers of Germanic speakers in what we call Scotland, as well as those who came over to Britain as Roman legionaries, the majority of these tribes do appear to have spoken forms of that P-Celtic tongue. Scholars have long tried to differentiate political and/or ethnic realities in Early Britain by what language they presume people spoke, but a shared language would be no guarantee of friendship or commonalty of purpose between members of tribes who were not directly related. This is important to understand as it helps us realise that the peoples who spoke the Celtic languages in the 1st Millennium the Picts, Britons, Cornish and Bretons and the Q-Celtic speakers round the Irish Sea had no concept of either a shared Celtic or national identity. We might better think of this period as one where there was a variety of linked and sometimes related tribes, some of whom used common languages. Having said that, there is no doubt that many of those who share a language share other aspects of culture. In the case of the North Brythonic speakers this means that they all seem to have had their own versions of the story of Arthur. These stories would have been known and understood by all of the different tribes. Just as the P-Celtic speakers had the stories of Arthur and his companions the Q-Celtic speakers had tales of Finn MacCoul and the Fianna, his warrior band. Both were the focus of whole series of heroic stories and poems though and there is evidence pointing to a degree of commonalty.

The role of oral transmission in pre-literate societies is complex but we can be sure of certain things. The stories they told were more than entertainment for the times spent round the hearth fires in the long months of winter. The transmission of information, how the world was formed, who you are, where you come from, how to deal with the world you inhabit, and how you relate to other people are all aspects of what we today call education and that education is driven primarily by books. Before books, such information had to be passed on via the spoken word. And that spoken word was often in the form of story. In all human societies stories form the basis of mythology and eventually religion, as well as giving people a version of their own particular history. Because of this the stories told to children in particular were told within the environment with which they were familiar. This helps make the stories more relevant, more meaningful and easier to understand. Thus the stories of Arthur told in Wales, Cornwall, Brittany and Scotland are all as real and valid as each other. They were part of the cultural inheritance of all of the groups that told such tales, none more so than any other. I have written elsewhere about the battles the possibly historical Arthur fought as being most probably located in Scotland, but the tales of these battles belong just as much in other areas.[6] The probable historical location of Arthur's battles in southern Scotland is something to which we will return because in some of the Grail romances we find what appear to be references to Scottish locations.

Nowadays it is accepted that the idea of the Anglo-Saxon invasion does not bear serious historical analysis. As John Koch puts it:

> It is fundamentally wrong, and in fact ludicrous to conceive of the English settlements and expansion as a great war of some 300 years in duration in which a monolithic British nation purposefully resisted the advance of a comparable monolithic German invader.[7]

If Arthur wasn't fighting invaders, whom was he fighting? I have suggested elsewhere that he was involved in a struggle between a militant form of Christianity and the pagan tribes who resisted it. I shall return to this point but it is worth stressing that the locations for the battle I suggest, following the nineteenth-century historian WF Skene and the writer JS Glennie are all close to what would appear to have been centres of communal tribal activity.[8]

Arthur if he existed, and there is still argument about this, would have been the leader of a war-band, akin to those raiding bands that were endemic in tribal society but perhaps he was a war-band leader with a difference. If he was involved in what was effectively a Christian crusade, his ongoing importance within the different oral traditions may well have stemmed from the fact that Christianity was triumphant in Britain. This would have made him a suitable hero for the tribal peoples who was useful to a Christian church intent on spreading its message, and power. The stories about Arthur appear to have formed an important if not central body of material within the cultural inheritance of the speakers of Archaic North Brythonic and as that language retreated into Wales so the corpus of tales went with it. Some stories however continued to be told in the north and are linked to various Arthurian place names in parts of Scotland where the dominant language became, over time, Scots, a language related to, but not derived from English. There are also similar motifs in stories from the Q-Celtic Gaelic tradition in Scotland and some of these motifs might well be older than the Arthurian tales themselves.

It is these traditional Arthurian tales themselves that underpin the writings of Geoffrey of Monmouth. Geoffrey was a teacher at Oxford in the middle of the 12th century and his name appears on a couple of local charters from 1129 and 1151. He was a cleric and in 1153 he was elected bishop of St Asaph in Wales, dying a couple of years later. Before writing *Historia Regnum Britanniae*, the *History of the Kings of Britain* in the late 1130s, Geoffrey had already completed *Prophetiae Merlini*, the Prophecies of Merlin, which clearly shows familiarity with the traditions of the Welsh-speaking people. Whether or not he was himself of Norman descent there is no doubt that he shows a certain sympathy for both the Cornish and Breton peoples, both of whom were P-Celtic speakers. The Normans under William the Conqueror, who invaded England in 1066, had been accompanied by a considerable number of Bretons. Geoffrey in fact suggests they were historically part of the great empire that he claimed had been created by King Arthur. He also gives us the utterly spurious descent of British kings from the Trojan hero Brutus in what we now see as an attempt to use the similarity between Brutus and Britain to give a Classical sheen of authenticity to his tale.

This attempt at obtaining respectability by reference to the Classical or Biblical tradition has led over the centuries to a great many spurious histories being presented for various British peoples. Such an approach is understandable from the point of view of someone brought up within the Church, for whom the power of that church, and the necessary triumph of Christian belief over all other creeds were unquestioned. However Geoffrey took a series of stories that had originated in a much earlier, pagan time and in presenting them to his audience he seems to have had no fear of invention. Apart from having his hero defeat the Saxon hordes of the non-existent Anglo-Saxon invasion, he has Arthur fighting the Picts and Scots, which does seem likely. However he also says that Arthur went to Gaul to defeat the armies of Rome! It is also from Geoffrey that we get the concept of the Machiavellian magician Merlin, and he later wrote *Vitae Merlini*, the *Life of Merlin* which draws substantially on traditional material. The book he claimed he had been given by his patron, Walter, the archdeacon of Oxford, was supposedly a collection of such material. Merlin himself seems to be based on a possibly historical character, the bard Myrddin who was at the battle of Arderydd in 573. This is according to the Welsh Triads, a series of Welsh verses, which have several references to Arthur even if the earliest manuscripts of them that survive are no earlier than the 13th century. Myrddin was fighting alongside Gwenddolau of Cumbria against Rhydderch of Strathclyde when the former was killed. It was this death that was said to have driven Merlin mad and he fled to live in the woods of Celidon, a clear form of the earlier term Caledonia. Nowadays Myrddin is seen as being one of a series of figures from both P and Q-Celtic tradition known as the Wild Man of the Woods and it is possible that the earliest of these is in fact Lailoken, who occurs in a Life of the Scottish saint Kentigern who supposedly also lived in the 6th century.

Wherever Geoffrey got his material, from an old book or from listening to the storytellers and bards of his own time, and however fanciful we now realise so much of his History to be, there is no doubt to its effect. For centuries Geoffrey's interpretation of the Arthurian material was an accepted part of pan-European culture and was used by amongst others, the Plantagent Kings of England to advance their own political agenda.[9] Shakespeare took the stories of such figures as King Lear and Cymbeline from Geoffrey, further spreading the influence of these re-told stories. We have seen that when the first printing press was set up in Britain by William Caxton it didn't take long for him to put *Morte D'Arthur* into print. This reflects the ongoing attraction the Matter of Britain and how it continued to inspire new compositions. One such work was *Sir Gawain and the Green Knight* written anonymously around 1400. This was only one of several pieces to appear in the medieval period on this theme in both England and Scotland. The roots of this story, like so much Arthurian romance, go back to sources that have survived in the Welsh language, though Gawain's father was said in several of the French and English Romances to have been Lot, king of Lothian and Orkney.

While such a personage seems unlikely to have ever existed as a historical figure, his specific location on Traprain Law in East Lothian, one of the important centres of the Gododdin, clearly locates him within a culture that knew of Arthur the warrior. The basic story underpinning Gawain and the Green Knight is that a giant Green Knight arrives at Arthur's Court and offers to let himself be beheaded by any knight present, on the condition that a year later he can then behead the knight. Sir Gawain is the only one to accept the challenge and when he has beheaded the stranger, the Green Knight picks up his head and leaves reminding all there of the promise that Gawain has made to undergo the same ritual. This tale has been interpreted as being very old indeed and possibly related to a ritual of renewal and regeneration as it is set at Midwinter. In the course of accepting his fate Gawain undergoes several temptations which he resists, before being released by the

Green Knight in his earthly form after simply touching Gawain's neck with the edge of his axe. Gawain survived temptation and it is this aspect of temptation and redemption that came to mean so much as the idea of the Grail Quest itself developed. However once more we have the location of basic Arthurian material in an undoubtedly Scottish context. One of Lot's other sons was Modred, Arthur's final foe.

In early Welsh literature there are many references to the Gwr Y Gogledd, the Men of the North and these references are to the P-Celtic speaking peoples we nowadays think of as the Gododdin and particularly the Britons of Strathclyde. It is also noteworthy that Traprain Law is one of the sites linked to the motif of the Nine Maidens that occurs several times in Arthurian material and is linked to similar ideas over much if the globe. I have written about this elsewhere but it is worth noting that these Nine Maidens also appear to be linked to other important Scottish hilltop sites like Stirling and Edinburgh Castles and Dumbarton Rock, traditionally the capital of the emergent Kingdom of Strathclyde and a site, like Stirling and Edinburgh, with its own specific links to Arthur. Tradition tells us that Arthur's son Smervie Mor, was in fact born in the Red Hall on Dumbarton Rock and Arthur is linked to Dumbarton in the Welsh Triads.

The links in traditional story between Scotland and Wales are considerable; Kentigern spends some time in exile in Wales, the northern chieftain Cunedda took a warrior band to Wales to fight off Irish invaders and supposedly founded a dynasty and a whole host of Scottish locations occur in the works of Taliesin and other early poets. I have noted that there are good grounds for seeing the battles fought by Arthur – according to the 8th century monk Nennius – as having been in Scotland. Scotland was never effectively under Roman control, was Christianised later than southern Britain and thus remained a pagan tribal society for much of half a millennium later than the country south of Hadrian's Wall, and these factors combine to suggest that something in Scotland was of primary importance in the development of Arthurian story and the idea of the Grail itself.

CHAPTER THREE

Arthur's Battles

Arthur's Battles – pagan sites attacked – importance of hilltop sites – notable locations – heroes and legends – Highland clan system – ancestor worship – Arthurian locales – sleeping warriors and kidnapped musicians – fertility/ femininity – tribal not national loyalty – idealised hero

THE LOCATION OF ARTHUR's battles has been the subject of much investigation. The general assumption on the part of most commentators is that he himself must have belonged to the area where the majority of these battles were fought. Claims have been advanced for Wales, Cornwall and northern England and also for southern Scotland. In my own book *The Quest for Arthur* I suggested locations for the battles mentioned by the Nennius in his *Historia Britonnum*. I believe that these locations themselves can help us understand how the idea of the Grail itself originated. I based my interpretations extensively on the works of WF Skene and JS Glennie that have been mentioned already. Glennie suggested the possibility that the list of battles that Nennius gave might well have survived till his time in the form of a poem. As we now know how extensive the use of poetry was in the warrior traditions of the 1st Millennium peoples this is an idea I believe is well worth considering.

Nennius lists the battles as Glein, Dubglas in Linnius, Bassas, Cat Coed Celidon, Fort Guinnion, City of the Legions, Tribruit, Agned and Mount Badon with four of the battles taking place at Dubglas. Most commentators have taken the order as given by Nennius but if Glennie is right then the battle order may well have been altered to fit a rhyme scheme. So, in considering the list I looked at the possibility that the battles were part of a single continuous campaign. The locations suggested by Skene and Glennie are that Glen refers to the River Glen in Ayrshire, Dubglas to the River Douglas in Glen Douglas running west from Loch Lomond, Bassas to Dunipace near modern Falkirk, Cat Coed Celidon to somewhere in the Borders, Fort Guinnion to the village of Stow in the hills south-east of Edinburgh, the City of the Legions to Dumbarton Rock, Tribruit to the shores of the Forth in the Carse of Stirling, Agned to Edinburgh Castle Rock itself and Mount Badon to Baden Hill just south of Linlithgow. A re-ordering of these could suggest a route that went from the river Glen in Ayrshire, through the Borders via Peebles and Innerleithen to Melrose, north through Stow to Edinburgh and from there west to Linlithgow, then through Dunipace near Falkirk on to the Carse of Stirling and finally to Dumbarton. This would leave only Dubglas to be accounted for. However heading east from the River Glen in Ayrshire towards Peebles there is another Douglas Water, a river that feeds into the Clyde south of Lanark. Could this perhaps have been the Dubglas referred to by Nennius?

As the Douglas Water runs some fifteen miles from its head-waters near Glenbuck Loch to its junction with the Clyde, while Glen Douglas is considerably less than half that distance in length, it struck me that there was more likelihood of four separate battles taking place along the length of the Douglas Water in Lanarkshire. It would also clearly fit in with the idea of a concerted military campaign passing through the Border hills then north towards the Forth. It was then that something in the landscape came to my attention. The Douglas water runs past Tinto Hill, a name that is said by some to have come from the Gaelic word *teintach* meaning 'place of fire', though there is a Welsh word *tanio* meaning fire. Tinto, the highest hill in the locality, has long been known to have been a site for the ritual fires of Beltain, and probably Samhain, or Halloween. These were the great feast days of the ancient agricultural year when communities gathered to celebrate and worship. It is the highest hill in the area and can be seen from many miles away.

It then struck me that if this was the Douglas referred to by Nennius the proximity to a place of sacral significance might in itself be important. Could the mention of the River Glein relate to something of similar significance? It runs past Loudon Hill, a prominent outcropping of rock in a flat plain and thus was a possible likely site for similar festal activities. Was this true of any of the other suggested locations of the battles? Apart from Stow which is in a narrow valley, though there is evidence of a mounded structure in a nearby glen, most of the others locations for the battles suggested by Skene and Glennie do seem to be in locations with notable hills. Edinburgh, Dumbarton and Stirling are all prominent rocks which have been important sites from prehistoric times. Dunipace or Bassas as Nennius referred to it, is actually named for two artificially enhanced flat-topped conical mounds and there are several likely candidates in the Borders for such a site that could be Nennius's Cat Coed Celidon. The most notable of these is perhaps the Eildon Hills, famously where Thomas the Rhymer entered the Otherworld with the Queen of the Fairies, and inside which a group of ancient warriors have long been said to lie sleeping, awaiting the hour of the country's greatest need when they will arise again. This is a recurrent motif throughout Britain that often specifically mentions Arthur and his knights.

The likelihood is that all these sites were used for communal rituals of one kind or another in pre-Christian times. A further relevant point might be that near Loudon Hill, Tinto, the Eildons and Dumbarton there are Roman forts. We know from the Romans that the inhabitants of what we now call Scotland had no cities and lived in small scattered groups in forest and by rivers. Dio Cassius tells us that the Caledonii and the Maetae 'possess neither walls, cities, nor tilled fields'.[10] However we do know that the native peoples created large and often complex structures on the tops of notable hills. Earlier interpretations which saw these as nothing more than the military encampments of high-status aristocrats no longer stand up. Many such sites are too large to have been of any military use and as I point out in *The Quest for the Nine Maidens* many of them including Dumbarton, Edinburgh and Stirling Rocks have associations with what appear to be pagan priestess groups. We should then perhaps think of such sites as centres for large-scale communal activities, whether sacred, social or economic where the dispersed populations would gather at significant times. Given that many of them also have a range of traditional stories associated with them they would also have held symbolic significance for the people using them.

The tribal societies of 1st Millennium Scotland were capable of uniting against invaders as the Romans make clear and they were also capable of working together to create massive stone and earth structures on these hilltop sites. They were the natural foci in the landscape, were associated with religious practice and were the sites of the great feasts when people came together from quite wide distances. This might not have happened every year – we have plenty of evidence right up to just a couple of centuries ago for local sites for the Beltain fires for instance – and might have been used only for particularly large or important functions, or on rare, significant occasions. Such sites might also provide suitable locations for other functions such as the annual allotment of land within the tribes – a practice that survived into late medieval agricultural practice – the settling of land disputes and the trying of criminal cases. They would also provide the natural places for particularly important marriages and funerals and possibly various kinds of initiation ceremonies. In addition they could serve a military function other than defence, in that they would be the natural muster points for the gathering of the warriors of the tribes in time of trouble, something echoed in later clan practice when the fiery cross summoned the warriors to the clan muster point. I would go further and suggest that mounds like the two Basses at Dunipace, like others at Inverurie in Aberdeenshire, St Vigean's near Arbroath and many others might have been artificially sculptured to resemble the outcroppings like Dumbarton, Edinburgh and Stirling, at least symbolically. We will return to this point. They would also provide the logical place for the Romans to focus on as they were the most likely spots where the native tribes would assemble their forces to resist them. From the Romans point of view they would also be the nearest things to political/administrative centres for the dispersed tribal peoples.

I have suggested that these sites could have been the focus of Arthur's campaign in that he was arguably a Christian warrior leading what amounts to a crusade against pagan sites of significance.[11] If he was leading a Christian crusade against possibly resurgent paganism after an earlier process of Christianisation in the 5th century led by St Ninian as is said to have happened, this would have made him a suitable hero figure for the new religion.[12] As an exemplary warrior he would hold his place within the oral tradition, as a model for all aspiring warriors but a hero who represented the new religion. This may be why he became such a universal figure, providing a link with the heroic figures of the oral tradition and the new literate Christian present. It is a noticeable aspect of the oral tradition that one hero can replace another, in a similar fashion to how stories are located within the known environment of the audience. In storytelling terms, what works survives, what doesn't, disappears. In the case of the hero there are clear instances of what were once Wallace's Caves becoming known later as Prince Charlie's

Caves and it seems more than likely that the figure of Arthur itself subsumed earlier heroic figures amongst the P-Celtic speaking tribes. We may even have an instance of this process on Tinto Hill where we have Wallace's Seat, which might earlier have been Arthur's Seat, a name which occurs in several Scottish locations. Next to Wallace's Seat on Tinto is Pap Craig a name of some significance that we will come back to.

The model of the Highland clans can perhaps help us understand what life would have been like for most people in Scotland up to the 7th or 8th centuries CE. We should also remember that the term pagan originally had the meaning of local or village and that this attachment to locale is echoed in how we understand oral transmission was utilised within the local environment. The focus of life was the kin group to which the individual belonged, which in turn was a component part of a larger tribal aggregation. This pattern survived in the Highlands under the clan system, and reflects an interplay with the local environment at both individual and community level that is much more immediate than the norm in modern society. This relationship with the landscape tied to what we can discern of what was religious belief makes the landscape itself a part of such belief at what is really a visceral level. It was a part of every individual and every community that was absolutely fundamental and implicit in everything they did. The relatively modern concept of the difference between the sacred and the profane would have meant nothing to such people, surrounded as they were by an environment in which they believed their ancestors to be still living on some level. In his *The Pagan Religions of Prehistoric British Isles*, Professor Ron Hutton suggested that it was likely there were specific rituals carried out at chambered cairns where priests effectively prayed to the ancestors to help seeds planted in the earth to grow into the following year's crops. Given the size of some the massive chambered cairns in Scotland dating from the megalithic period, it is also perhaps worth considering whether their mounded shapes had a symbolic significance echoing prominent hills.

Part of the evidence that led Skene to locate Arthur's battles in Scotland was the fact that there are Arthurian place names and traditions that have survived in different parts of the country. These include Ben Arthur at the head of Loch Long which also has *Agaidh Artur*, a face that can be picked out in nearby Glen Kinglas. West of Lanark there is Arthur's Craigs and to the north of Biggar is Arthurshiels Farm, while in the Rhinns of Galloway, where according to the Welsh Triads, Arthur had a fort, there is Arthur's Slunk, slunk meaning a muddy place or hollow. In the borders south west of Dumfries there is Loch Arthur. Another place name in Morayshire is perhaps worthy of mention here. Near Lossiemouth on the Moray coast there is an Arthur's Bridge and less than a kilometre to the south west there is Caysbriggs. Cay would appear to refer to Kay or Cei who is traditionally one of Arthur's closest companions. Close by these places there is an ancient earthwork which might have been in use in the 1st Millennium. The linking of different legendary characters within the same part of the landscape also occurs elsewhere, notably at Meigle where apart from Arthur's Fold, Arthurstone and Arthurbank there is Vanora's (Guinevere) Mound and, on nearby Barry Hill, Mordred's Castle. The idea of Arthurian place names as far north as the Moray Coast is hardly surprising if one accepts that the P-Celtic speaking Picts who inhabited much of Scotland throughout the 1st Millennium also had their own Arthurian traditions.

There are several Arthur's Seats, one on Ben Arthur itself, another south of Peterhead, *Suidhe Artair,* a Gaelic form, near Dumbarton and one on the north end of the Isle of Arran, a favourite hinting ground of the mythical Gaelic hero Finn MacCoul. There is also an Arthur's Seat on Hart Fell, near Moffat in the Scottish

Borders where Alexei Tolstoy located Merlin's Cave in his *Quest for Merlin*. The best known of these though is Arthur's Seat in Edinburgh which to this day people are insisting is nothing to do with Arthur. The explanations given are either along the lines of David I renaming it because he had read Geoffrey of Monmouth's *History,* or that it derives from a Gaelic term referring to arrows – *saighead* – linked with the word for high or height *"ard"*. This despite the fact that Edinburgh is mentioned in the poem containing our earliest reference to Arthur, *The Gododdin*, and the Gododdin were P-Celtic, not Gaelic speakers. It seems the idea that Arthur simply **couldn't** be Scottish has taken a firm root, as have so many interesting, even quaint notions regarding the Grail itself, despite what common sense would suggest.

There are many other Arthurian place names in Scotland and JS Glennie has extensive lists of these and other names that crop up in *The Mabinogion*, the poems of Taliesin and other early Welsh literature. This simply reinforces what we know – that the people in these areas were, like the medieval and many modern Welsh people – speakers of a P-Celtic language. There are also stories told about Arthur, including the one at Meigle where local tradition says that Queen Vanora, the local name for Guinevere, was buried in the kirkyard after having been torn to death by a pack of wild dogs. This was said to be a suitable punishment for her treachery to her husband and people. In this version of the story Arthur actually appears to be Pictish and the story is linked to a particularly magnificent Symbol Stone in the wonderful wee museum there. This magnificent Class II Pictish Symbol Stone – which has extrusions which show it to have been part of a composite monument, unique amongst such stones – has the alternate interpretation that it represents the Christian Biblical story of Daniel in the Lion's Den. Given that remnants of pagan practice survived till at least 17th century in Scotland it seems at least possible that back in the 1st Millennium some of the Symbol Stones could be interpreted in terms of both Christian and pagan traditions. Another story of Arthur is referred to by Donald A Mackenzie in *Scottish Folk-Lore and Folk Life*.[13] He tells us that there was a tradition of Arthur sleeping with his knights below Arthur's Seat in Edinburgh. As we have seen another of these stories concerns the Eildon Hills, telling of the horse trader Canobie Dick who came into the vast hall where warriors were sleeping, fully armed with a fully equipped horse by each warrior. On a table lay a horn and a sword in a scabbard and he was told by his guide that if he chose correctly whether to draw the sword or blow the horn first he would become the leader of this mystical force and a great hero in his own right. He blows the horn first which turns out to be the wrong decision a great voice booming out, 'Woe to the coward that ever he was born, Who did not draw the sword before he blew the horn.' The unfortunate Dick survives only long enough to pass on his story before dying on the slopes of the Eildon Hills. Though the warriors under the Eildons are not specifically referred to as being Arthur's knights, they seem to fit the pattern and it seems likely that in the past this story could have referred directly to Arthur.

While there have been suggestions that this type of tale – like those of musicians spirited away into fairy hills – is a memory of rituals at chambered cairns, Dick's failure to make the right decision is reminiscent of something else. When in *Perceval* the hero reaches the court of the Fisher King in the Land of the Grail, the latter is suffering under an enchantment which keeps him apart from the rest of humanity. When the marvels of the bleeding lance and the Grail are paraded before the pair of them, Perceval's failure to enquire what these marvels signified, meant he was unable to loose the Fisher King from his enchantment. This idea recurs in several of the Romances and in the 13th century German *Parzival* by Wolfram von Eschenbach it is made explicit. Parzifal initially fails to ask the question that will cure the king, Anfortas but after further adventures returns and asks the question 'What ails the King?', thus allowing the Grail to heal the king. The Fisher King is wounded in the thigh and this has been generally understood as a reference to sexual impotence and in Parzifal he is explicitly wounded in the genitals. On a symbolic level the injury refers to the fact that the Land of the Grail is itself arid and barren. This sterility can only be lifted once the king is cured and this motif harks back to the truly ancient idea of the sacred king who is symbolic of the land itself. Within the traditions of the Celtic-speaking peoples the land was represented by a Queen who the king has to marry to achieve his role. This concept of the femininity of the land, and its link to the Grail as a specifically feminine symbol will be looked at later.

The phallic symbolism of the bleeding lance is clear and just as there seems to be an underlying ancient reality concerning the turning of the seasons in the tale of Gawain and the Green Knight, in the Romances of the Grail there is likewise an underlying reality, deriving from originally pagan traditions that concerns the idea of fertility, and the linked concept of regeneration. The turning of the season and the great feasts of Beltain and Samhain in pre-Christian times were of course directly tied to the idea of ensuring ongoing fertility for crops, animals and humans.

It is important to realise that in such a society the figure of Arthur as an ideal of the supreme warrior could be of major importance without the need for him having to be a king like figure. As late as the 17th century most people in Scotland outside the Highland areas lived in small communities, fermtouns, which were similar in social organisation to the clachans in the Highlands. People lived in groups of a handful of families holding the land in common with the best, and worst, land being shared out between all.

This appears to have continued the pattern of scattered small communities that had been noted by the Romans. Even when kingship was well established, at least in the Central Belt and eastern coastal area in the early Middle Ages, the courts of the kings moved around the country. Their control over distant parts of the country like the Borders, Dumfries and Galloway and the ever problematic Highlands and Islands took centuries to be established. The idea of loyalty to a nation state, or a distant king, came very late to such areas.

Back in the 1st Millennium the role of the warrior was central to society but as a part of the community not separate to or apart from it. Everything we know about such societies from Roman descriptions through to 18th century reports, tells us of societies that were bound by unbreakable bonds between the members of the group. What has been seen as the exclusivity of tribal behaviour is also, from the point of view of the members of the tribe, inclusive. Within later Scottish clan society the concept of the 'broken man' allowed those rejected from one group to join another as long as they accepted the rules and took the name of the group they were joining. While clan society, like the earlier tribal system was always fluid and adaptable, certain underlying realities were taken as read. These were the ties of blood and mutual interest. Even into the present day in crofting areas of Scotland people come together to work on projects of shared benefit without having to be told to do so by some person of supposedly superior social standing or higher authority. They do this because they still behave like people in the old tribal societies. You know everybody, you are probably related to most people in the community and there is universal advantage in using the opportunities provided by being prepared to work communally. The work and the benefit are shared. There is also the human awareness in conservative societies that something that has worked in the past, will work in the present. This applied also to matters of ritual and magic. Though Scotland has been seen as universally Christian by no later than the 7th century and possibly earlier, this did not prevent the ongoing use of what were essentially pagan rituals of healing and devotion well into the 19th century in many parts of the country. As late as the 17th century there was at least one instance of animal sacrifice in order to counteract cattle disease (See Chapter 9 note 1), showing that people will hang on to ideas that they think will work.

This idea of Arthur as an ideal warrior amongst the P-Celtic speaking tribal peoples of Scotland seems perfectly natural. We know that the function of the warrior at the heart of society continued in Highland society up to and beyond 1746. That was the year of Culloden when the Jacobite army of Prince Charles Edward Stewart, Bonnie Prince Charlie, was finally defeated not far from Inverness. After the battle there was widespread brutality by the victorious British Army throughout the Highlands as the long term ambitions of both Scottish and British governments to rid themselves of the dangerous clans at last became possible. The adherence to the old tribal ways of blood-ties, and raiding had been infuriating kings to the south for hundreds of years. In many ways we can see that society as being a development of the type of tribal structure that had existed in the time of Arthur. Even after Culloden groups of men who had 'been out' on the Jacobite side carried on a sort of guerrilla warfare by reverting to the traditional custom of cattle raiding. Now however they were not raiding the cattle of other clans, but exclusively those of Lowland farmers, many of whom they saw as legitimate targets because of their support for the British Government, and their Protestant religion. There had always been sporadic raiding on the Lowlands but now, with the entire Highlands destitute because of the actions of the rampaging British Army these men focussed their activities, and often their hatred, on the Lowlands. They knew their time had passed. But in this last desperate stand they were still harking back to the idea of the warrior that lay at the heart of clan society just as it had in the tribes that inhabited Scotland in the time of Arthur.

We have seen that the evidence strongly suggests the story of Arthur was known amongst the Pictish tribes, who were, at least in cultural terms, cousins to the Gaelic speakers of the west and their fellow P-Celtic speakers south of the Forth-Clyde line. The idea of the warrior-hero was close to the heart of traditional story and belief in all of these societies. It is then worth considering whether some of these Pictish Symbol Stones like the one at Collessie on Fife which has a single warrior on it, might refer to some such idealised warrior-hero or even god-like figure based on the same idea. There were a number of other Pictish Symbol Stones that had a single warrior on them, which have mainly survived as fragments, the ones we know about being in Fife, Angus and Aberdeenshire on the east coast of Scotland. Probably the best known is the Rhynie Man, a fierce looking character with filed teeth! While it is impossible to know whether one or more of these individual warriors was ever referred to as Arthur it does suggest that there was an awareness of a particular individual warrior who was considered extremely important, so it is perhaps not beyond possibility that such portrayals could have been of Arthur, or someone like him.

Whether the Arthur who fought the battles described by Nennius was an actual figure is perhaps not capable of being proved absolutely. What is absolutely certain is that amongst the tribal peoples of Britain there was a clear idea of a heroic figure called Arthur around whom a vast corpus of traditional material gathered. One interpretation is that there was such a warrior in the 6th century who took his name from an earlier, legendary figure, something that has been known in many human societies down the ages.

The name Arthur itself as been suggested as linked to the bear, a totemic creature in many early societies, and there have been suggestions that many Arthurian place names are close to pre-historic alignments to the Pole Star, which is of course part of the Great Bear constellation. Such ideas are again not susceptible to proof, but suggest that in the figure of Arthur who is said to have lived and fought in the 6th century, we can see links with ideas that are of even greater antiquity. The universal Christian heroic king that has inspired artist, writer, poets and musicians for well over a thousand years is himself a link to continuities of ideas that stretch back into the far distant past.

CHAPTER FOUR

Quests and Questers

Idea of the Quest – The Grail as Chalice – Lancelot and Galahad – roots in P-Celtic tales – Gawain – Traprain Law – early Scottish saints – Bride in Scotland – suppression of feminine role – shamanism – symbolic cauldrons – Rosslyn and Templar fantasies – Avalon – Glastonbury

IN *The Hero with a Thousand Faces*, Joseph Campbell made the point that religions are often created round a heroic figure. In this context he specifically mentions Buddha and Moses as having overcome a series of obstacles to achieve their final status. He suggests humans have a recurring need for such heroic and transcendent figures and we can clearly see that Arthur conforms to this type of heroic figure. The tribal warrior societies of 1st Millennium Britain, like their own ancestors, would have had many tales of heroes and their gods would have been modelled on them. However with the introduction of the Grail concept into the Arthurian material the heroic figure took yet another turn. In the figure of Chrétien's *Percival* the mystery of the Fisher King's court is introduced and Robert de Boron developed the concept further by bringing in the idea of the Grail as a chalice-type object itself. This provided a focus for the hero's quest in many of the following Romances, that, though it was mysterious, even supernatural, was suggested to be a physical object. Thus the Grail Quest was something that was being presented as being achievable for humans who, though heroes were not necessarily transcendent or potentially superhuman. In the series of knights who seek the Grail in these Romances we can see them being presented as a more accessible form of Campbell's idea of the Hero, with whom the intended audience could identify. Just as mythology explains our existence and the world we inhabit in terms of beings who resemble humans, and gives rise to codified ideas that grow in to organised religions, so legends are told to provide examples and models for how we should behave. In the pre-literate world children were taught how to behave in society through stories of people behaving in ways that were presented as being acceptable and also in stories which clearly showed the results of behaviour that was not acceptable. This is the basic idea behind 'moral tales', which in time were presented in literature like the Fables of Aesop.

While we have mainly looked at the idea of the hero through the figure of Perceval this far, and he is either based on Peredur in *The Mabinogion*, or is drawn from the same source, there are better known heroic figures generally associated with the Quest for the Grail. Probably the best known of these today are Lancelot, Galahad, and Gawain, all of whom played a major role in the Romances of the 12th and 13th centuries, though in the tale of his encounter with the Green Knight, Gawain's story seems to echo ideas that were already ancient by the time of Christ.

Lancelot who first appears in Chrétien de Troyes' *Erec*, a name clearly derived from the Scandinavian Eric, does not seem to have been based on any particular figure in early Welsh literature. He was the most popular of the Arthurian knights amongst the French writers as Lancelot du Lac, son of the King Ban of Benwick. This location, otherwise given as Benoic has been linked to Bannock, a place name best known in the Battle of Bannockburn when Robert the Bruce defeated the Invading army of the invading Edward of England. The burn rises in the Campsie Fells which formed the northern boundary of the Strathclyde Britons and which have a series of possible Arthurian locations at their western end. Before he went to England to join King Arthur's knights he was closely associated with a female fairy, known as the Lady of the Lake, a creature that harks back to an earlier and widespread mythological creature who crops up in Welsh oral tradition. At Arthur's court he becomes a favourite of the queen Guinevere, with whom he comes besotted, mistakenly sleeping with one of his many female admirers in the belief that she was Guinevere. It is the son of this union, that in the end prevents Lancelot from attaining the Grail. Despite the supposed high moral tone and chivalrous concepts associated with Arthurian Romance, when the opportunity arose, Lancelot wanted to have sex with Guinevere, the wife of his King. As always, reality seems to break through, as if the underlying mythological and legendary material can not be kept down. In another of the Romances *The History of the Holy Grail*, he does manage to sleep with Guinevere and when their adulterous affair becomes known and she is imprisoned he rescues her, though he ends up in a nunnery and he ends up being banished back to France. In this tale Lancelot is killed and his severed head is thrown into a well. This echoes a series of tales within the British Isles where severed heads are associated with wells, and may perhaps be linked to the story of Bran's severed head. Lancelot occurs in a local oral tradition at Edenhall near Penrith in England, where he killed a giant called Tarquin.

He also appears in a Scottish poem *Lancelot of the Laik*, which was based on earlier French works and did not appear until the 15th century. Two other Scottish Arthurian Romances are known, *Golagros and Gawain* and *Sir Gawan and Sir Galeron of Galloway* from the same period. The influence of Geoffrey of Monmouth in particular might be the reason that Arthur, Modred and others appear in several medieval Scottish chronicles. Just as the earliest Annalists were influenced by Classical and Biblical sources, so the medieval Chroniclers drew on earlier texts. Before the invention of printing, texts had to be copied by hand and were extremely valuable objects and perhaps because of this their contents could be treated with too much respect. The idea that because something is written in a book means that it is true, is one that we perhaps have not yet put behind us. We know that Arthurian traditions survived in Scotland but it is unclear to what extent these chroniclers were influenced by Geoffrey's writing and how much by still extant tradition within their own contemporary culture. Traditional stories are tenacious.

Sir Galahad first occurs in the Vulgate *Quest of the Holy Grail* written in the early years of the 13th century and it has been suggested he was modelled on *Gwalhafael* in the *Mabinogion* story of Culhwch and Olwen. He is Lancelot's son by Elaine of Corbenic who posed as Guinevere to lure Lancelot into his bed. Galahad does fulfil the Grail Quest in that he manages to cure the Maimed King, a variant of the Fisher King. He also attains the Grail and in his search for the great Truth underlying the Christian idea of the Trinity he drinks from the Grail and he is whisked off to heaven. Put another way, he achieves his aim and dies. His birth is said in the Vulgate *History of the Holy Grail* to have been organised by his grandfather Pelles, who with the assistance of Arthur and others seeks to bring into being the knight who can fulfil the Grail Quest and thus restore fertility to the land. This is in itself strongly reminiscent of Geoffrey of Monmouth's story of how Uther Pendragon, masquerading as of Duke Gorlois of Cornwall with Merlin's help, seduced the Duke's beautiful wife Igraine and impregnated her with the child who was to become Arthur.

Sir Gawain was as we have seen, said to have been the son of King Lot of Orkney and the Lothians. Whether or not Lot was based on a historical figure the linking of the Lothians and Orkney clearly suggests that he was Pictish. The Pentland Firth is accepted as referring to the Picts so we can assume the Pentland Hills in the Lothians have the same meaning. Gawain possibly derives from the figure of *Gwalchmei* in the Welsh traditions, who features in the story of Peredur. Lot is presented in the writings of Geoffrey of Monmouth and others as being married to Arthur's sister Morgause. He is elsewhere said to be the father of Thenaw, who gave birth to the Scottish Saint Kentigern after her father first had her thrown off the top of Traprain Law in a chariot, then set her adrift on the River Forth in an oarless boat. He was trying to punish her for refusing to marry after she was seduced and made pregnant with the future saint. Such was her holiness however, despite having been seduced, by a prince from Strathclyde, that she survived both episodes because of divine intervention. As in many early biographies of saints there is as much magic as in the earlier pagan stories, though by explaining it as divine intervention the monks writing these tales could keep their consciences clear. Traprain Law was an important site in the land of the Gododdin, has associations with a Nine Maidens group and is a prominent hill in flat plain. Gawain goes on a quest to find the Holy Grail but his fiery temper is instrumental in him failing to reach his goal. He dies after a battle with his one-time friend Lancelot, though he has time to forgive him before succumbing to his wounds. Interestingly Gawain was said to be intensely curious and his curiosity grew stronger every day till noon, and began to fade after the sun went down. Given his role in the story of the Green Knight and its mid-winter setting, Gawain certainly seems to retain some aspects of a much earlier and truly mythological figure. It is also noteworthy that we see links between the originally pagan figures of Lot and Gawain and one of Scotland's earliest saints Kentigern, said in Jocelyn's *Life of Kentigern*, to have met with Columba who was conducting his Christian mission amongst the Scots and Picts from his base on Iona in the West of Scotland.[14] Iona had been a sacred spot before the arrival of the Christians and as it was a deliberate policy of the Christian Church to take over pagan sites to preach the new Gospel, it would seem natural to also take over some of the legendary or mythological figures known to the local people and Christianise them. That this was done with figures like Bride, who in Ireland became St Bridgit and separately became St Bride in Scotland is well attested. There seems no reason to doubt that this is the same ancient goddess figure of the Brigantes, the British tribe living in the north east of England when the Romans arrived.

I have looked briefly at these three figures to illustrate the idea of the Quest for the Grail. Only one of the three actually found it, but the search for it is clearly represented in work after work as being a great adventure for those who wished to prove themselves true heroes. While the Grail is presented in the various Romances as a sacred object, imbued with Christian mysticism, there can be no doubt that the idea of the heroic quest and the Grail itself developed from underlying ideas which came to Geoffrey of Monmouth, Chrétien de Troyes, and the others from much earlier ideas. These ideas originated in the oral traditions of the P-Celtic speaking peoples in Britain, with parallels in the closely related Q-Celtic traditions. And in Scotland in the 1st Millennium we had both P and Q-Celtic speaking peoples.

It is notable that in the whole of the Matter of Britain, while female characters are occasionally presented as motivating forces, the action revolves around the males. The whole focus of the tales in both the Early Welsh sources and the later Romances is King Arthur himself though the action is often undertaken by others like Galahad, Gawain and Lancelot. In her *Gods and Heroes of the Celts*, Marie-Louise Sjoestedt makes the point that 'the religious notions inherited from the classical world have such a hold on the imagination of western man that we have difficulty not introducing them, even when they are out of place.' She goes on to say that because of this there has been a tendency amongst scholars to fit what we learn about other cultures to the model of the Greek Pantheon of Gods. The point has already been made about all our earliest texts being written in monasteries by monks but it is also important to emphasise that they were all men. We have no record of early Annals or records coming from nunneries. Sjoestedt's suggestion can be seen as a justification for being somewhat critical of the supposed construction of both Irish and Norse myth, with their overwhelmingly masculine set-up. The Early Welsh material though not thought of as presenting a similar Pantheon of Gods, bear the same hallmark. Those whose actions matter are male, women do little more than motivate them, though as an example the figure of Cerridwen in the poems of Taliesin, is clearly based on a powerful mythological female character. Her links to the Nine Maidens suggest that she is in fact a memory of a Mother Goddess figure if not that Goddess herself.

The Christian obsession with sin, and the effective demonisation of women that resulted, ensured that such figures were unlikely to be sympathetically treated by the monks who were keen to put on paper the traditions and stories of the people to whom they belonged. These female characters, apart from their dangerous femininity were also clearly pagan and the Christian church was regularly beset with crises of heresy. Paganism was even worse than heresy so we can have some sympathy with these early recorders of indigenous tradition.

However before we consider this in detail, we should look further at the Grail Quest and at some of the other strange notions that have arisen around the Grail, notions that also appear to be concerned solely with the actions of men. In light of 'received knowledge' about the past, it is all too easy to stress the role of heroic or even supernatural masculine figures but this is something that might well be a hindrance to our understanding rather than a help. There are varying ways of interpreting the material that has come down to us from the past. As we will see much of what seems to be the oldest type of sacred thinking focussed round the idea of the world having been created by a divine female.

In fact some people have interpreted the Grail as a specifically female symbol. Jean Markale the professor of Celtic Studies at the Sorbonne in Paris was one of these. While his *Women of the Celts* is perhaps overly influenced by Freudian psychological interpretations, he does make some telling points. He suggests that the Quest itself was originally a pagan rite and that it was driven by a desire for vengeance by blood. However he thinks that this was only part of the story and directly compares the idea of the Grail Quest to both Otherworld journeys which occur in many cultures, and to shaman practice where the shaman goes on journeys to the spirit world. He also notes that in the Procession of the Grail in its various representations there is clear phallic reference to the bleeding spear while the Grail itself can be interpreted as representative of the female vulva. It is the combination of these two elements he suggests that allows the devastation of the Land of the Grail to be overcome and fertility restored. He thus sees the Grail as an essentially feminine symbol and in its connotations of fertility and regeneration notes that it can be compared to the idea of the magic cauldron that occurs in early Irish and Welsh sources, and in Scottish tales The cauldron is central to the understanding of where the deepest ideas of the Grail can be found, as we shall see. Cerridwen of course had a magic cauldron which is said to have been tended in one case by a group of Nine Maidens and on another by the boy Gwion Bach who as a result of his task goes through a clearly magical initiation. We shall come back to the cauldron, as so many have done before.

Increasingly in the modern world the idea has developed that it is the search itself that is the point, not the success in finding a particular object. The cliché is that it is the journey not its end that is important. By putting himself through the trials his Quest brings him, the Hero is tested and strengthened. It is as if nowadays we are trying to understand the symbolism of the Grail in a more personal sense that we can apply to our own lives. Nowadays personal disciplines like yoga, tai chi and the various martial arts based on ancient Eastern philosophies flourish as do esoteric religions and some belief systems that to non-participants seem plain silly. Religions have always been about organisation, control and ultimately power, and though many modern religious systems clearly follow this pattern there is no doubt that a great many people see themselves as being on their own personal quest. Whether that Quest is for religious or philosophical enlightenment, a better state of physical health or simply a means of self-improvement, the idea of these journeys seems ever more popular, at least for those who can afford the time or money to follow them.

The attraction of the old Arthurian tales and the idea of the attainment of the Grail fits into this pattern, particularly alongside both new and supposedly re-discovered ways of seeing the world that are generally called New Age. A quick visit to your local bookshop's ever growing section on Mind, Body and Spirit will show you this. If you are lucky some of my books might even be there. Here I should declare my own interest. It is through my own research into ancient pagan priestess groups and the history of my native Scotland, particularly in the 1st Millennium, that I first became involved in looking at Arthurian material and the ideas which are presented in this book are a result of what has at times felt like my own personal Quest. I am not of a mystic turn of mind at all but sometimes eerie things have happened and it has at times felt as if I was being led. By what, or whom, I cannot be sure.

Although the idea of the spiritual Quest has grown more and more popular, the last couple of decades have seen an upsurge of interest in the idea that the Grail is there to be found. In fact with the current publicity about the book the *Da Vinci Code* and its alleged origins in ideas expressed in *Holy Blood, Holy Grail* interest in the idea of the Grail has never been higher. And yet again Scotland figures largely. For some time there has been an idea going round that Rosslyn Chapel to the south of Edinburgh is an important location for those who seek to find the Grail. This idea has been developed because of the supposed involvement of the builder of Rosslyn Chapel with the Templars. Well he was involved with them, but not in the way that has been presented. The Knights Templars were a Military Order founded by the Christian Church in the aftermath of the First Crusade. This had taken place in 1096 and was successful in wresting control of Jerusalem from the Saracens who had taken over the city in the 7th century. Now that the city was under Christian control it was expected that there would be a constant stream of Christian pilgrims to this, their holiest city. In order to protect these pilgrims and Jerusalem itself, the Poor Fellow-Soldiers of Christ and of the Temple of Solomon, commonly known as the Knights Templar were formed. From their very inception we can see that there was en element of wish-fulfilment about the organisation for no matter how deeply people believed that they had rediscovered the Temple of Solomon mentioned in the Christian Old testament, there is no real evidence that they had, certainly by modern standards of scholarship. However belief is a powerful force and the slaughter of thousands in taking the city of Jerusalem to reintroduce a religion formed round the words of a man who preached love, was not considered odd.

In order to support the work of the Knights Templar they were given lands all over Europe by the Church, kings and lesser aristocrats. Over the next couple of centuries the organisation became extremely rich and powerful. They were a common sight around Europe with their distinctive white surplices with a red

Maltese Cross and it has been estimated that for every actual fighting Knight the order had ten other members supporting him, as farmers, artificers, farriers, bankers and all the other functions needed to support them. They were generally considered the finest fighting men in Christendom. There was however a problem. They were all monks, and unlike many other clerics in the Middle Ages they were celibate and were very much a closed order. It was clear that their primary loyalty was to one another. They were effectively an independent army throughout the whole of the Christian world and though their declared role was the defence of Jerusalem their power in different countries was such that they became perceived as a danger by various kings and in time, even the Pope. Their independence, their separate command structure, their great fighting prowess and their increasing wealth undoubtedly made them a threat to established powers. So when the hammer fell there were many ready to act against them.

In 1307 the French King Philip IV moved against the Templars. The Holy Land had been lost to Saladin's armies at the end of the 12th century and subsequent Crusades had proved unsuccessful. The role of the Knights Templar, and brother organisations like the Knights Hospitaller, in defending and supporting pilgrims to the Middle East no longer existed. Yet they still preserved their structures, their power and perhaps most significantly, their wealth. Philip IV of France had tried to bring the Templars and Hospitallers under his own direct control but failed. He was also in financial difficulties and had his eye on the lands and wealth of the Knights. Over the next few years the power of the Templars was broken absolutely. In 1307 Philip moved against them, arresting hundreds of Templars and having them charged with a variety of crimes These included that they denied Christ, committed sacrilege, indulged in obscene acts, worshipped idols and used criminal acts to further their or order's wealth and power. Guilty verdicts were inevitable, and some of the charges might even have been true. In 1312 the Pope Clement V officially a disbanded the order and they ceased to exist. By this time the Templars had been stripped of their possessions and put on trial in much of Europe and those of their number who were not arrested, tried and often executed, were absorbed into other monastic orders. Scotland was no different. In 1309 the Templars on in Scotland were put on trial and it is significant that Sir William St Clair of Rosslyn and his cousin Henry testified *against* the Templars.

The fantastic stories that have arisen abut Rosslyn Chapel are expertly dealt with in *Rosslyn and the Grail* by Mark Oxbrow and Iain Robertson and a couple of points should suffice here. People try to claim that the gravestone inside the Chapel is a Templar one. This is like the equally spurious notion that the sword-graves of the Western Highlands and Islands of Scotland are all Templar – there is absolutely no evidence to support this idea. The symbol of the wheel headed cross on the Rosslyn grave slab is a well known form of cross associated with St Catherine of Alexandria and the St Clairs had built a chapel dedicated to her in Glencorse before Rosslyn was constructed. Much has also been made of the number of 'green men' carved all over the chapel. This is not particularly unusual, Dunblane Cathedral for instance has considerable numbers of them, all in open view. The suggestion is that these are a pagan symbol and thus a link with pre-Christian beliefs, with the hint that they symbolise some truly ancient mystery. In fact they were a common medieval form of adornment particularly in Italianate chapels and part of the symbolic imagery available to the men who designed and built Rosslyn for the St Clairs.

The whole link with Templars is a late invention and owes its origin to fantasies of the latter-day Knights Templar who are an offshoot of Masonry, that once Radical organisation that now is shrouded in secrecy and probably corruption. However this is not to say that Rosslyn is totally irrelevant in searching for the Grail. It is not the Chapel that has significance but its location. It overlooks Roslin Glen which contains rock carvings, including spirals and concentric rings which might well date back to at least the Bronze Age. These specific symbols and their location within a secluded glen and opposite a cave carved into the living rock, all speak of ancient sanctity and as we shall see there is considerable evidence in Scotland's landscape which points towards the origin of the Grail. The Glen is like several other locations in Scotland in that it is a deep cleft in the landscape containing what are clearly marks of ancient sanctity and ritual.

The linkage of the idea of the Grail to Rosslyn is dependant on a series of misreadings of history and downright fabrications, as Oxbrow and Robertson show, but this is not the first time that such ideas have been used. The current exploitation of the tourist trade by the trust in charge of Rosslyn Chapel is well-intentioned. The preservation of such an architectural treasure in a country where so much Christian history was destroyed in the fanatic vandalism of the Scottish Reformation is to be commended, but any long term spiritual significance there is linked to the glen. There are those who will say, with some justification, that such sites build up sanctity because of the visits they attract. I have long considered myself a hard-headed realist but was moved to tears on seeing the Statue of Liberty, I presume because the feelings of hope and joy experienced by millions of people on seeing it for the first time have in some way imprinted themselves on that great statue. Or maybe I too am gullible. However exploitation of tourist interest in King Arthur and the Grail, though it would not have been understood in those terms, has a long history. In the closing years of the 12th century the monks at Glastonbury announced to the world that they had discovered King Arthur's grave. Monasteries near sights of pilgrimage have always been

prosperous and the attraction of King Arthur was well understood by the monks of Glastonbury. In 1190 they dug up a coffin
containing the bones of a large man. Beside it was a lead cross
with a Latin inscription which translated said, 'Here lies the
famous King Arthur, in the Isle of Avalon.' At a stroke they had
the body of Britain's most famous hero and declared their own
location to be the mystical Isle of Avalon. This was the island
Geoffrey of Monmouth had claimed Arthur was taken to after
his last fateful battle with Modred at Camlaan. The island itself
is linked to very old concepts of the Island of Women and the
Land of Everlasting Youth that existed well beyond the so-called
Celtic world. The monks' claims were clearly based on Geoffrey
of Monmouth's work and there is little doubt nowadays that the
cross at least was a forgery. It is however ironic that Glastonbury
is in fact a good candidate for an ancient sacred location, perhaps
even an Island of Women in pre-Christian times.[15] This of course
makes it an ideal location for telling the various stories about
Avalon. Given that we know it was Christian policy to take over
sites of earlier religious practice this, like the ongoing attraction
of Rosslyn Chapel is perhaps not surprising.

However at Glastonbury there was a further development to
what appears to have been a truly enterprising piece of sleight of
hand by the monks. Robert de Boron's *The Chronicle of The
History of the Grail* had introduced the idea of Joseph of Arimathea
bringing to the West, specifically to 'Avaron', the cup which Christ
had used to perform the Last Supper. It was a simple matter to
claim that this in fact referred to the Isle of Avalon that Geoffrey
of Monmouth wrote of and thus the claim that Glastonbury was
the Isle of Avalon made it the location of the Grail itself.

CHAPTER FIVE

Ancient Roots

Importance of The Mabinogion – Bran's severed head – cauldrons of rebirth – votive offerings – the Carlin and the Cailleach – fairies as ancestors – Cerridwen and Taliesin – links to Stone Age – cauldron as a symbol – Pictish symbols – deer as symbol – Glamis Manse stone – Christian re-usage of sites

THERE IS LITTLE DOUBT that Chrétien de Troyes was working from either the story of Peredur as it occurs in *The Mabinogion* or the same source that the original compiler of that collection of tales drew on. *The Mabinogion* is the name used for the collection of tales preserved in the Welsh language that were taken from two very early books. These were the *White Book of Rhydderch*, compiled around 1300-1325, and the *Red Book of Hergest* put together a little later in the period 1375-1425. Though these were compiled after Chrétien's time there is little doubt that they were based on extant oral traditions which seem to have come from much earlier. Without going into too much detail the stories that were brought together in *The Mabinogion* were of the same type as Geoffrey of Monmouth was drawing on for his Life of Merlin and at least some of his Arthurian stories. It is impossible to date these types of traditional stories other than by what they tell us of themselves, but scholars have no doubt that the Welsh stories in *The Mabinogion* do reflect traditions that were already very old before they were put into literary form. *The Mabinogion* tales – like similar material from Ireland that survives in literary from the early medieval period – preserve clearly pagan material. Given that we know story can hold on to provable data in some instances for upwards of thirty thousand years, it is likely that some of the motifs that occur in these early literary sources might be very ancient indeed.[16] These motifs then went on to influence many writers over a geographical area well beyond the British Isles.

In both Chrétien's *Perceval* and *The Mabinogion* story of *Peredur, son of Efrawg,* the hero comes to a castle and is sitting in conversation with an older man when a procession enters the chamber. In both cases a long white lance is being carried in the procession with blood running from its tip, and in both cases the hero does not ask his companion what this marvel means. In *Perceval*, two boys carrying golden candlesticks are followed by a maiden carrying the Grail, while in *Peredur*, two maidens follow the spear carrying a great salver or plate between them. On the salver was a man's head in a pool of blood. In neither instance does the hero ask what these marvels mean. This is significant because it was only by asking what they meant that the hero would initiate the process by which the King would be healed of his wound, and that fertility would return to his lands. It seems as though Chrétien has substituted the Grail, a chalice, for the severed head. The severed head itself is probably a reference to another of *The Mabinogion* tales *Branwen, Daughter of Llyr*. In this tale Bran, clearly a god-like figure, here called Bendegeidfran, has his head cut off by his friends after he has been wounded by a poisoned spear. Under the influence of Bran's severed head his seven companions spend the next years at a magical feast lulled by the song of three magical birds after which time they buried the head under the White Hill in London, latterly the site of the Tower of London. From here the magic power of Bran's head was said to have protected the island of Britain, against all invaders. In Wales a late story tells of Arthur digging up Bran's head because he resented there being any defender of Britain but himself. This was said to have preceded the so-called Anglo-Saxon invasion, the hint being that this act precipitated it. And as we have seen there was widespread tradition linking severed heads and wells.

However in the story of Peredur the hero comes across yet another magical object which is directly linked to Bendegeidfran or Bran. At the court of the King of Suffering, Peredur sees dead warriors being brought into the castle and restored to life after being bathed in a tub or cauldron. This appears to be the same as the cauldron given to Matholwch, king of Ireland by Bendegeidfran. Bendegeidfran tells Matholwch in *Branwen, Daughter of Llyr*, of 'the virtue of the cauldron is this: a man of thine slain today, cast him into the cauldron, and by tomorrow he will be as well as he was at the best, save that he will not have the power of speech.'[17] This could hardly be more specific – the cauldron restores life.

Many commentators have suggested that at least part of the idea of the Grail as a transcendent mystical object derives from such ancient traditions. Lewis Spence who wrote extensively on myth, legend and folklore in the first half of the 20th century said: 'According to folk-lore theory, the belief in this vessel was derived from the assumed existence of the magical cauldron of a Celtic fertility cult.'[18] He goes on to suggest the idea of the Grail developed in Britain from traditions of the indigenous peoples, was transported to France by the early Middle Ages and then developed independently as the interest in the Matter of Britain flourished throughout much of Europe. This notion that the Grail developed from a grafting of Christian idea onto what had been an important pagan fertility symbol – the cauldron – has much to commend it. Spence was not alone in making this link. Rees and Rees in their *Celtic Heritage* make the following point about cauldrons, 'these vessels of life and plenty may be classed with the Holy Grail of medieval romance'.[19] Cauldrons crop up in many different traditions and even in early sculpture in Scotland. Professor Jean Markale made this specific point in his *Women of the Celts*:

> We should also remember that one archetype of the Grail is the famous ritual and magic cauldron that appears throughout the legends of the Celtic islands. Its significance merits careful study.[20]

Cauldrons certainly crop up in early Welsh literature. Cerridwen's cauldron is looked after by Nine Maidens who themselves seem to be a memory of group of pagan priestesses that existed in many parts of the world. There is also a linked idea in early Irish literature where the cauldron of the Dagda, themselves seen as Irish Gods, was capable of feeding a host, nine at a time, though it would not boil the food of a coward. The Dagda is generally considered to be the most senior of the *Tuatha de Danaan*, the Father of the Irish Gods. This cauldron is also linked to fertility and regeneration, showing the idea was widespread throughout the British Isles. It is also intriguing to consider the Gundestrup Cauldron, a magnificent silver object found buried in Denmark in 1891. It had been disassembled into the silver plates from which it was originally made perhaps as some kind of votive offering. There are reasons, apart from the close contact that has always existed between Britain and Scandinavia for asking whether it could have been made in Britain, not least the men blowing the war-horns or carnyxes, one of which was found in Morayshire dating from around the 1st century CE. The symbolism of the images on this cauldron can in fact be linked to traditions amongst both Celtic and Germanic speaking peoples of north-western Europe. Given what we now understand of the close contacts between peoples in this part of the world in the past, it was perhaps made in Denmark itself by people who were part of a cultural world in which ideas were not limited by the language they spoke.

Cauldrons also show up elsewhere. The throwing of offerings

into wells, rivers and lakes as offerings to gods or spirits is well-attested in many societies throughout the world, a practice known as votive offering. One particular hoard of such offerings dating from around the 1st century CE, was found in Carlingwark Loch near Castle Douglas in Dumfries and Galloway in 1886.

Amongst the hoard was a large iron cauldron. This cauldron is currently on show in the new Museum of Scotland and it is noticeable that the simple ring-type decoration on parts of it are very like the discs on the nearby Pictish Symbol stones and the rings on Stone Age carvings on the other side of the gallery. The name of the Loch Carlingwark, derives from Carlin, a hag-like figure who occurs in Scots traditions in various guises, including that of a landscape creator and is a precise match for the Cailleach, or Hag of Winter who occurs in Gaelic tales. The Carlin has also been interpreted as the Queen of the Witches and the association of witches with cauldrons, in which they supposedly brewed up their potions, is well known. In passing, the idea of Macbeth consulting the three witches round their cauldron in Shakespeare's play, is actually supported by local tradition that talks of Pictish kings consulting wise women at a stone circle just north of Aviemore. In the parallel figures of the Carline and the Cailleach we see ideas surviving in different language traditions alongside each other, suggesting an original common origin.[21]

Lewis Spence said this in his *The Magic Arts in Celtic Britain*, 'The Grail cannot be anything else than the cauldron of abundance and inspiration so frequently alluded to in ancient Celtic literature.' He mentions the examples from *The Mabinogion* and others in Irish tradition before turning to one which is particularly significant. This is the magical cauldron which Arthur goes to Annwn, the Welsh Underworld, to fetch. This is described in the poem *Prideu Annwn,* the Harrying of Annwn, which is attributed to Taliesin. This cauldron is kept in the fortress of *Caer Sidi,* which probably means the Fortress of the Fairies and only seven of Arthur's force return from the assault. Hugh McArthur, the Historian of the Clan Arthur, has suggested that if we accept the Gododdin as being a document referring to an actual historical event, then why not the Harrying of Annwn.[22] He suggests that here the 'fairies' are probably nothing other than pagan Picts or possibly even Scots. The reference here to Sidi which is very like the Scottish Gaelic *Sìdh*, meaning the fairies might suggest something else. Many of the ancient chambered tombs dating from thousand of years ago were known to the Gaelic speaking populace as *sìdh*, here meaning fairy mounds. This raises the intriguing possibility that the term Caer Sidi might refer to a site that was already understood as being of very ancient sanctity in the 6th century. We know that ancient sites like stones circles were the locales for various rituals into historical times, so the possibility that Caer Sidi was so named because it had been known to be a sacred site for a long time is certainly not impossible. We know that the tribal peoples of Britain considered their dead ancestors to be very important, and as I have noted, there have been suggestions that they prayed to them. In this context a site that had been used to contact the ancestors over an extended period could easily become associated with the *sìdh*, and some commentators have gone so far as to actually suggest that the Fairies were in effect these ancestors. The priests or druids who officiated there and those who perhaps protected them could thus become fairies themselves, at least in the eyes of the Christians, Arthur and perhaps Taliesin.

Arguments have raged for a long time as to when Taliesin was writing. Some people think he was around at the time of Arthur in the 6th century, while others have suggested he lived hundreds of year later but drew on the same body of material that had inspired earlier poets. In *Prideu Annwn* the cauldron he mentions is said to be Cerridwen's, the one that was tended by nine maidens.

In another early poem *Hanes Taliesin*, the History of Taliesin, this was the cauldron that Cerridwen, a goddess figure in her own right, was using to brew up a magic potion. The brewing had to continue till the contents of the cauldron were distilled into three drops which would have the power of conferring total understanding on whoever drank them. Cerridwen's intention was to give this gift to her son Avagddu as a compensation for his being extremely ugly. The three drops would give knowledge of the past, present and future. Tired of watching over the process she entrusted the cauldron to the care of Gwion Bach, a little boy. However the three drops spilled from the cauldron and fell on Gwion's finger. They were of course boiling hot, so he automatically put his finger into his mouth and sucked it, taking in the drops of magic essence. Immediately he understood everything, and realising he had thwarted Cerridwen's plan he fled. She senses what has happened, returns and gives chase. Then there follows a remarkable series of events in which Gwion Bach, using the knowledge he has gained, shape changes into a series of creatures.

First he changes into a hare, then a fish and a bird. In order to try and catch him, Cerriwden likewise changes into a greyhound, an otter and a hawk. At last he turns himself into a grain of corn at which point Cerridwen changes into a hen, pecks him up and swallows him. Nine months later she gives birth to Gwion Bach. She cannot now bring herself to kill him so, in a motif that is echoed in stories from many lands, she casts him adrift in a basket. He is found by another mythical being Gwyddno Garanhir, who names the foundling Taliesin, Shining Brow. He then grows up to be the greatest Welsh bard of all time. In the references to shape shifting people have discerned references to shaman practice where the shaman undergoes a spirit journey during which he or she changes into animal form to commune with the spirits and in other stories of the Nine Maidens, they too are shape-shifters.

I have elsewhere noted that the Nine Maidens occur across many different societies and language groups on most continents, and can perhaps even be seen in the Magdalenian cave painting from el Cogul in Catalonia. Here nine women are seen dancing round a priapic male figure in what clearly seems to be some sort of fertility rite. This dates from at least fifteen thousand years ago. We are here dealing with a truly ancient idea and it is well to remember that in many cultures the cauldron itself is a powerful symbol for very practical reasons. Even today a cauldron usually sits over the fire in the centre of the tents of nomadic peoples and is thus the focus of family or community life. In the 1st Millennium before people started to build stone houses with gables for the fireplace, houses had their fire in the centre of the floor with a smoke hole above it, echoing the practice in the tents of their ancestors. This was where food was cooked and people often ate around the fire over which the cauldron hung. There can be no doubt that its long-term associations with the notions of fertility are rooted in its everyday functions. It was useful as a symbol because it was universally known and experienced. It also has a strong link to story because it was round the fire, particularly in winter, that storytelling took place. Also, because of its location it was physically at the centre of all activities that took place in the home. The combination of this centrality with fire and food made the cauldron an inescapably powerful and universal symbol for thousands of years.

The importance of the cauldron as a symbol can also be seen on the Symbol Stones of the Picts. The cauldron occurs on several of them as a symbol and one of them in particular underlines the cultural links and similarities between the different groups of P-Celtic speaking tribes. This is the symbol stone outside the old manse, or minister's house at Glamis, a place associated with Macbeth and the site of one of Scotland's more magnificent castles.

Glamis also has its own local Nine Maidens and Early Christian traditions. On one side of the Symbol Stone there we see a salmon and an adder, corresponding to the earliest form of the Pictish Symbol Stones, dating from the pre-Christian period. What are known as Class I Pictish Symbol Stones are simple, unshaped standing stones with incised or pecked symbols, usually a pair of them, on one side and they are considered pre-Christian, or pagan. Class II stones are shaped stones, which have symbols, and sometimes Biblical or hunting scenes on one side and Christian crosses on the other. They use relief carving as well as incision, while the Class II stones are magnificently ornate Christian monuments that incorporate some Pictish symbolism. The Glamis Manse stone is unusual in that it appears to be an originally pagan stone which was later shaped and sculpted with an ornate Christian cross and a series of symbols on the other side. A couple of the symbols on the cross side are particularly interesting. One of them is the head of a deer, but the way it is portrayed suggests it may in fact be the representation of a mask – deer masks are known to have been used in rituals for millennia and at Abbots' Bromley in Staffordshire in England, the ancient deer dance still takes place annually on the first Sunday after 4 September. The other symbol of interest is a cauldron, seen from the side – most Pictish cauldron symbols appear as seen from above – so there is absolutely no doubt as to what it is, and sticking out of it are two pairs of legs. Suggestions have been made that this is a reference to some kind of Pictish ritual drowning, but the evidence that this ever took place is non-existent. What I would suggest we are seeing is precisely the same thing as was described in *The Mabinogion* tales, a cauldron of rebirth. This is understandable in the light of shared cultural motifs between the Picts and the P-Celtic speakers of southern Scotland and beyond, which are shown by the geographical spread of Arthurian place-names and stories.

These links go back to the period before the Romans arrived in Britain and the strongest recurring idea here is that of fertility and regeneration. The Grail itself is clearly a symbol of regeneration and in the comments of writers like Jean Markale and others, the feminine aspect of its symbolism also suggest fertility. In the 1st Millennium and earlier these ideas of fertility were of central importance. The advent of winter meant that food had to be stored up and given the fragility of human life it was necessary to appeal to the gods and/or spirits for assistance to ensure that the crops which had been planted would grow and ripen. This is similar to the practices we know from around the world where hunter-gatherers make supplications before going out to hunt animals. Life was fragile and even if crop-growing peoples had more security in their food sources than those relying on hunting and gathering, they were still at the mercy of the weather. In today's world we see recurrent famines due to changing weather patterns and though many of these might be as result of over intensive farming, the use of essentially poisonous fertilisers and general environmental degradation, the reality is that for many people throughout the ages, famine, or extreme hunger was a constant fear. This meant that the ideas of fertility were central in rituals and beliefs, and thus in the symbols associated both with the rituals and the myths and legends that accompanied them. Mythological figures are presented in essentially human form, though with supernatural powers and often of gigantic size, because this makes them understandable and thus approachable. The symbols used in ritual practice like-wise tend to be rooted in actual experience and in the cauldron we see this clearly. Its links to the Grail preserves a truly ancient continuity without it being offensive to the Christian church.

However, even after the Christian church became dominant in the whole of Britain, there is no doubt that many of the ancient ideas and even practices of pre-Christian belief continued. I have already mentioned that early Christians in Britain re-used what were older ritual sites and this was deliberate policy. Bede in his *A History of the English Church and People* quotes a letter, sent in 601 CE from Pope Gregory to Bishop Mellitus as he set out for Britain to spread the Christian message. Gregory tells the bishop, 'to destroy the idols but the temples themselves are to be aspersed with holy water, altars set up, and relics enclosed in them'.[23] It is somewhat ironic that idols are to be replaced with relics and he later says to take over their animal sacrifices as Christian Festivals. The main point here is that Gregory recognises the need for continuity. This policy in fact appears to echo the storyteller's location of his tales within the known environment of the audience. In both cases the intent is to make the absorption of the 'message' easier. I have already pointed out that particular locations were chosen for what appears to be large scale sacred and social functions within the tribal peoples of Scotland and it is noteworthy that just as the oldest surviving building on Edinburgh Castle Rock is St Margaret's chapel, many churches in Scotland are built on mounds, mounds which perhaps served precisely the sort of social and sacred functions within tribal practice as would have occurred at Edinburgh, Stirling, Dumbarton and other locales that were ritual centres for the surrounding peoples.

CHAPTER SIX

Continuities and Contacts

Surviving fire-festivals – wells – sacred numbers –
storytelling exists alongside literacy – cultural contacts –
Scottish references in the Grail Romances – P-Celtic survivals
– over reliance on language as a mark of ethnicity – links to
Europe – continuities since Megalithic period – Scotland
Christianised late – origin of British

WE HAVE SEEN THAT the idea of the Grail as a cauldron of fertility
and magic is based on very old ideas indeed. Echoes of some of
these ideas still survive, as at Abbot's Bromley and in the various
fire festivals that occur in Scotland, particularly to celebrate the
New Year. Midwinter was always important, because from then
on as the nights shrink, Spring comes closer. All over the world
people now sing that great Scottish song Auld Lang Syne, and
often link hands and move forward and backward as they sing.
This is a truly ancient dance form and preserves a continuity from
the far past in the modern world because it makes the singing of the
song at this important time more of a communal event. And no
one doing it has ever needed to be told this. Throughout Britain,
as elsewhere in the world people are recreating what they think are
rituals based on these old ideas. Just a few hundred yards from my
home in Edinburgh the annual Beltain festival on Calton Hill in
Edinburgh has been taking place for nearly twenty years. While the
symbolism of much of the activities owes more to Mediterranean
than Scottish sources, the popularity of this event reflects a wider
phenomenon. The old practice of hanging rags by sacred wells has

resurfaced at wells and many other sites over the past few years all over Scotland. Some sites, like the Cloutie Well on the Black Isle north of Inverness possibly preserves an unbroken continuity of such behaviour since pre-Christian times, and it is serving as a model for people visiting other wells and ancient sites. This is because people wish to tap into what they see as the sanctity of these ancient places and connect with the planet we inhabit in a direct way that is impossible within the established religions.

A great many practices dating from pagan times have survived in what today are called superstitions. One personal instance should serve to illustrate this. If two things went wrong in our house when I was child, say something had been spilt and something else had been broken, my grandmother would always break a matchstick because she said bad luck came in threes. This may well be linked to the widespread triple repetition of acts at wells and other sacred sites that is so widely attested in folklore. Sometimes of course this went further and in the three times three or nine repetitions we see something that has cropped up in many societies – the idea that repetition a set number of times made the ritual more effective. Three and nine were (are?) believed to be especially effective. It also linked to very ancient beliefs like those in Norse mythology which says that the universe exists in nine worlds, which is itself similar to Chinese thinking. However the use of three might be based, like so much of ritual practice, on observation. It is well known that one of the ways of remembering extensive lists of things is to link them in threes. Somehow this makes remembering things easier. This is precisely the sort of mnemonic, or memory trick that we can understand must have been part of the development of initiates like priests, bards and seannachies (genealogists) in tribal times. The need to rely on memory in pre-literate societies is obvious and it is again interesting to realise that well into the 19th and 20th centuries, folklorists came across people, from the

Balkans to the Hebrides, who retained poems and stories in their memories that took hours, and in some cases days, to recite or tell. Just as literacy did not consign the storytelling tradition to oblivion, so some of the techniques of pre-literate times continue to exist.

The reason for the survival of 'superstitions' is that the dominance of Christianity has never been absolute. The process by which Pope Gregory wanted to take over the pagan temples to ensure the grounding of Christianity might have helped already deeply rooted ideas to continue. In pre-industrial society, communities were much more conservative than they are today in that people often lived on exactly the same piece of land that their direct ancestors had, for hundreds, possibly in some cases, thousands of years. This meant that not only was there a deep emotional and social attachment to the land, perhaps in some ways akin to the territorial awareness of many animals, but also a situation existed where anything that had been believed to have been of benefit in the past would be retained. It is this process that is probably behind the animal sacrifice referred to above. For this to have happened someone must have not only believed that this would work as a cure for cattle disease, but at least one individual must have been privy to the actual necessary ritual behaviour. Continuities do not just exist within the storytelling tradition.

We have considered the Scottish provenance of much of Arthurian lore that, like such superstitions, might have arisen so far in the past as to be incalculable. While emphasising that this is in no way reduces either the cultural relevance or authenticity of Arthurian traditions in other locations, Scotland is particularly important in how the cauldron motif developed. Having noted the ongoing importance in Welsh tradition and literature of the Men of the North we must consider why this was. Certainly the links between the P-Celtic speaking people of Scotland and the rest of

Britain were integral to the development of those traditions and literature. The recent growing awareness of the importance of water transport in pre-historic times suggests that the cultural contacts, certainly between coastal people in the British Isles was extensive and continuous. The over emphasis on what language the various tribes spoke in the past has led to this being insufficiently considered and studied. Within the material that we refer to as the Matter of Britain, there is a clear aspect of harking back to the concept of a Heroic Age, certainly in the poetic and symbolic sense.

It is a recurrent theme throughout human history that times were better in the past, that the heroes of yesteryear were of much greater stature than anyone who now walks the earth and that our ancestors – always at a time in the past that is not specified – lived in some kind of Golden Age. This is an attitude on a societal level that echoes what happens with individual human beings who very often, as they get older, look back with fond remembrance at what they perceive as being better and happier times. This is simply nostalgia and it seems to have a role in society at large, and probably always has had. However in the references to the Men of the North and the various locations in what we now call Scotland in *The Mabinogion*, and many other Arthurian Romances, we are perhaps seeing something else.

One specific example can perhaps help us begin to understand this. In the 13th century the French Romance *Fergus* by Guillaume le Clerc which takes place in Scotland. In it, there is a description of Castle Dolour:

> It was situated high on a native rock. At its foot ran the river 'Hombre' on one side and on the other a large river which came from more than forty springs which poured through an arch at the base of the 'tower'. Within the 'keep' was what seems from the description to have been a chambered barrow later opened and re-used.[24]

I am unaware of any barrow having been located in the foundations of Castle Campbell above the small town of Dollar, but this description strikes me as pretty accurate of its situation. The Burn of Sorrow and the Burn of Care meet below the Castle, and the Burn of Sorrow flows from the east through a narrow gorge which does not have an arch over it today but it is possible there was one there in the past. The name Dollar is probably P-Celtic in origin from *dol*, meaning a valley and is mentioned in the Pictish Chronicle as the site of a battle in the 9th century. As Guillaume le Clerc chose to set his tale in Scotland it is tantalising to consider whether he had access to material that had originated there. This would perhaps explain why there is such a close correspondence between his description of Castle Dolour and Castle Campbell in the glen above Dollar. It is also tantalising to speculate that Castle Dolour might also have originally derived from *dol*.

This of course is not the only Arthurian site around the river Forth which flows eight miles or so to the south of Dollar. We have seen there are grounds for locating several of Arthur's battles around the river and Edinburgh Castle Rock is also firmly linked with the epic poem the *Gododdin*. In my *The Quest for Arthur* I have gone further and suggested that the Isle of May in the River Forth is a possible site for the Isle of Avalon to which Arthur was said to have been carried after the Battle of Camlaan by Morgan and her eight sisters. The locating of legendary locales within the known environment of their audience was as we know a common practice, but just as there are there are archaeological and historical grounds for locating the battles in this area I believe there are good grounds for suggesting the Isle of May as Avalon. Skene, followed by Glennie suggested that Camlaan was in fact the modern Camelon near Falkirk, near the south bank of the River Forth, which is central in the Scottish identification of several of Arthur's battles.

The Isle of May means the Island of the Maiden or Maidens and there are Nine Maiden traditions linked to other prominent Scottish sites we have considered such as Edinburgh and Stirling Castles, Dumbarton Rock and Traprain Law, a prominent site of the Gododdin. The Nine Maidens also survived in Scottish tradition as a group of Pictish saints. The Isle of May itself was both a site of pagan and Early Christian burial suggesting it was a sacred location long before the Christian religion came to Scotland. Nine Maidens also crop up in Early Welsh literature, including in the story of *Peredur* in *The Mabinogion* where they show up as the nine witches of Caer Lyow, a group of Amazon like figures who are defeated in battle by the hero Peredur, and Cai, another Arthurian 'knight' is said to have pierced nine witches in Ystavingon in the poem *Arthur and the Porter*. They are also linked to the goddess Cerridwen in the Taliesin poem *Prideu Annwn* where they are said to look after the goddess's cauldron of poetry and inspiration. This cauldron is clearly part of the tradition of the magical cauldrons that survived from early times in Britain. It is also relevant, that it is as part of a group of Nine Maidens, that the Cailleach, the Hag of Winter, rides out from Ben Nevis to bring Winter onto the land.[25]

The idea that the Arthurian locales in Scotland date from the time that P-Celtic was still being spoken from the Forth-Clyde line south to the border with England has been challenged. RS Loomis, author of many books on the Matter of Britain, suggests that the 13th century use of the term Castle of the Maidens for Edinburgh Castle, and other Arthurian references was the result of a whim by King David 1. The reason he gives is that because King David 1 knew Robert of Gloucester and that Robert of Gloucester was Geoffrey of Monmouth's patron, so David must have been given a copy of the *History of the Kings of Britain*. Loomis then suggests the king was so overwhelmed by Geoffrey's work that he renamed his capital and a series of other locations throughout Scotland, and that the rest of the population accepted this renaming. Others have taken up this assertion – based it would seem on Loomis's conviction that Arthur could not have been Scottish in any sense at all – to explain Arthurian place names and local traditions all over Scotland. This despite the indisputable fact that the earliest known literary mention of Arthur originates in a poem that no one disputes was written in or around that very Castle of Maidens in the 7th century, the *Gododdin*. However as we can see all too clearly with the development of recent ideas about the Holy Grail, people will believe what they want to.

The survival of Arthurian traditions in Scotland is clearly due to the fact that so much of the country was, in tribal times, part of the cultural milieu of the P-Celtic speaking world. Modern ideas of nation states with rigid borders drawn on precise maps combined with the odd concept that language is related in some way to ethnicity, has led to some dubious interpretations of the past. Part of the reason for the references to the Men of the North and Scottish locales in so much early Welsh literature might however be due to something that was in fact a rigid border. South of Hadrian's Wall the Pax Romana, the rule of the Roman Empire lasted for over four centuries. This has obviously had a considerable effect on the history and culture of England and Wales. It has led to the suggestion by many writers that Arthur, though now increasingly being accepted as essentially a tribal war-band leader, was in some way trying to carry on the system of law and order that had been known under the rule of Rome. Some writers have even suggested the same thing in Scotland. That would be very strange indeed for the Romans were in Scotland for an extremely limited time, certainly not long enough to substantially alter the tribal system that was the social norm here.

Though they first came into Scotland in the 1st century under

Agricola and continued trying to conquer the whole of Scotland until the late Severan campaign at the dawn of the 3rd century, and even after, there is no evidence that they ever established the Pax Romana north of Hadrian's Wall. Modern archaeology has shown that the Antonine Wall, from the Forth to the Clyde across the whole of Central Scotland was only occupied for a period of about 30 years. It was primarily built of earthen banks in contrast with Hadrian's Wall which was stone built. The Antonine Wall was abandoned around 186 CE and the frontier withdrew to Hadrians' Wall, which was itself subjected to attacks from the north regularly for the next two centuries. This tells us quite a lot. Around 217 the Roman author Dio Cassio wrote that the Caledonians, a term virtually interchangeable with Picts, lived right up to the wall, the closest tribe being the Maetae. Scholars have always considered the Maetae and the Caledonians to be essentially the same people. Dio Cassio, writing so long after the abandonment of the Antonine Wall and having been secretary to Septimus Severus who was in Scotland at the turn of the 3rd century, is unlikely to have made a mistake here. He is effectively saying that the Caledonians or Picts were the inhabitants of all of Scotland, with the Maetae closest to Hadrian's Wall. Scottish historians have tended to place the Maetae to the north of the Antonine Wall citing two significant place names, *Dumyat*, from Dun Myat, the Fort or hilltop place of the Maetae, just east of Stirling and Myot Hill a few miles to the south. Perhaps these names are similar to the widespread us of Inglistoun, English town and Scotstoun, found in many parts of the country. A similar example of this is Rathillet, the Fort of the Ulstermen in north Fife. These would all seem to refer to settlements of people from without the immediate area and were so called by the local tribal people. We know there was cultural interchange between different areas from megalithic times onwards so this should not be seen as surprising.

It is one of the unfortunate results of relying too much on linguistic evidence that historians have created the idea that if one language group was dominant in an area, it was the only language in use in that area. While this may make a handy theoretical construct for linguistic analysis it contradicts common sense.

When referring to the Caledonians or Picts the Romans must therefore have been including the Scots, the Q-Celtic speaking people of Argyll, whose putative arrival in 500 AD from Northern Ireland has been shown to have been be no more than a piece of medieval propaganda.[26] There is no evidence on archaeological or linguistic grounds for thinking that the Scots were not in Argyll when the Romans came and thus were probably part of the Caledonian army that faced Agricola at Mons Graupius. While the tribes of Dalriada, as the Scots territory was called, were Q-Celtic speaking, their society was essentially the same as that of the P-Celtic speaking tribes in the rest of what we now call Scotland, and the rest of Britain before it was conquered by the Romans. In later centuries the fact that 'kings' of both Picts and Scots came from the other group is a recurring fact, showing that despite the language differences they were able to work together, at least some of the time. The idea that they were clearly differentiated political societies before the seventh or eighth centuries seems somewhat far-fetched. They were tribal peoples. In the case of Dalriada we know they consisted of the Cenel Loarn, the Cenel nGabhrain, the Cenel nOengusa and the Cenel Comgall, Cenel here being an early Gaelic word meaning kin, and corresponding closely to the later term *clann*, meaning children. This term is significant in that it refers to the existent clan as being the descendants of a common ancestor but also has the sense of responsibility to the children to come. This is exactly the same process by which later clans named themselves, for instance MacGregors claiming descent from Gregor son of Alpin, King of the Scots in the 8th century,

MacLeods from Leod, son of Olaf the Black, brother of Magnus, last King of Man, and so on. We can perhaps better understand the social and economic structures of 1st Millennium tribes of Northern Britain by looking at later clan society. The loyalty of the warriors in such societies, and all able men were warriors, was to the tribe. The chief was the embodiment of the whole tribe and loyalty was to the tribe through him, not to him as an individual. This loyalty to the kin-group, tribe and clan, can be seen well into the Middle Ages in Scotland where the Lords of the Isles and their followers were capable of entering into treaties with Kings of England against the Scottish monarchy.

We cannot ever hope to untangle how the relationships between the various tribal groupings of early 1st Millennium Scotland worked out in detail but we can be sure that the idea of anything like a nation state was totally foreign to them. Being outside the control of Rome these tribes continued to function as they had done since the Iron Age and possibly earlier.

The supposed differences between the Picts, the Scots, the Gododdin and the Britons of Strathclyde can therefore be seen to be much less important than their similarities, certainly before the expansion of Northumbria in the 7th century which forced extensive and dramatic societal change. The Picts and Scots sometimes inter-married and at other times fought each other. This corresponds very well to what we know of inter-tribal behaviour at a more local level where raiding was endemic, even between clans who at other times might be allies, or even intermarry. This raiding tradition carried on in the Borders into the 16th century and in the Highlands into the 18th century. What tied these societies together was kinship not kingship. The capacity for Picts to rule Scots, Scots to rule Pict, Britons to rule Scots and so on is understandable within a tribal structure.

Over and beyond the immediate tribe there must have been

some sort of organisation allowing for both the reported massing of the Caledonians against Agricola at Mons Graupius and the massive confederation of tribes that assaulted Hadrian's Wall in 360. The Romans referred to this as the Barbarian Conspiracy and it consisted of Picts, Scots and Saxons. At first this seems surprising. Historians have always stressed the battles between the Celtic and Germanic speaking peoples. Yet again this is result of trying to define people by language, both ethnically and socially. Saxon is a rather vague term as used by the Romans, but undoubtedly refers to Germanic-speaking northern mainland European tribes. We know from the archaeology that people in Scotland had been in contact with people on mainland Europe since at least megalithic times in the 4th Millennium BCE and that this contact, however sporadic, lasted into historical times.

It is only in recent times that the true nature of sea-travel has begun to be understood. We have long known that the Megalithic culture included Spain, Portugal, some of the western Mediterranean islands, France, Holland, North Germany, Denmark and southern Sweden. The last four mentioned places could all be seen as being possible locations for the Saxon tribes who joined the Barbarian Conspiracy. There is no reason to doubt that contact between Scotland and these parts of the European mainland had been continuous since the time of the megalithic builders. It is after all just as possible to travel by boat from Scotland to Denmark, Friesland or the Netherlands as is it is to London, even if the later only involved coastal sailing. People had been sailing up and down the coasts of Britain and well beyond for thousand of years before the Romans came. This continuity of contact over the North Sea is underlined by the discovery of a timber hall at Balbridie near Montrose, dating from around 3,500 BC and conforming exactly to building styles in Holland and Germany at the time.[27] Similarly, finds of penannular bracelets and pins from a variety of locations have shown links to Scandinavia and northern Germany in the 7th and 8th centuries BCE.[28] This continuity of contact might have something to do with what we will see is the geophysical reality that underpins the symbol of the cauldron.

Because Scotland was outside the Roman Empire it seems likely the process of Christianisation took place differently there. It is also likely that whatever the original pagan beliefs of the British tribes were, they would have changed less in Scotland. Although the Romans were tolerant of all religions, the influx of legionaries from all parts of Europe and Africa – there were Moroccan troops manning parts of the Antonine Wall during its brief life – must have made a difference to how religion developed south of Hadrian's Wall in the 400 years of the Pax Romana, even before the entry of Christianity.

The Roman Empire itself became Christian in 389 when the Emperor Theodosius pronounced it the official religion and many pagan temples were destroyed or converted to Christian use. The religion had already been tolerated for over half a century within the Empire. The first of the English saints was supposedly St Alban who was said to have been martyred as early as 304 and the Emperor Constantine was converted a few years later which put an end to the Roman persecution of the Christians. The later traditions of the legendary Joseph of Arimathea as we have seen, claim he had arrived in Britain in the 1st century. There is thus some evidence for Christianity in England in the 4th century but there can be little doubt that north of Hadrian's Wall it had not as yet gained a foothold. I have suggested elsewhere that Arthur's battles can be interpreted as an early kind of Christian crusade against the pagan tribes of Southern and Central Scotland and it is not till the end of the 6th century that St Columba expanded the religion into the north of the country and there is little evidence for it having been dominant any earlier.

If Arthur was militantly trying to spread Christianity he would in this case be following on the actions of the Emperor Theodosius at the end of the 4th century, who was as brutal in pushing Christianity as many of his predecessors had been in suppressing it. It is safe to say that Scotland remained pagan later than England. It is also true to say that the Columban Church held sway over most of the country until after the Synod of Whitby in 664. There has probably been too much emphasis placed on the differences between the Columban Church, essentially controlled from Iona, and the Church in England which was effectively under the control of Rome. However as Scotland had escaped Roman occupation, the possibility must exist that the beliefs of many, if not most of the tribes, retained many aspects of earlier indigenous pagan belief well into what is generally accepted as the Christian era. Christianity in its early days in Britain was almost entirely an urban phenomenon and while England had seen substantial urbanisation under the Pax Romana this did not happen in Scotland. The foundation of St Ninian's settlement at Whithorn was probably not until the latter half of the 6th century and we can probably best see the growth of urbanisation of Scotland beginning under the direct influence of the Christian church, rather than as in the south of the island, being due to Roman civil organisation.

It can never be more than surmise, but after the slaughter of the Druids of Mona, now known as Anglesey, by Paulinus Suetonius around the year 60 CE, survivors may well have headed north just as earlier survivors of the Gaulish druids had supposedly headed north into Britain ahead of the Romans. This would be all the more likely if there was something specifically of major importance to the pagan religion in the north.

What cannot be doubted is that the people in Scotland remained non-Christian, tribal and almost exclusively rural, long after those to the south were subjected to considerable societal change. This can only have served to ensure a continuity not only of economic and social structure but of ritual and belief. Scotland was more conservative because it was less exposed to major change. There was change, the Romans tried on many occasions to conquer the northern part of the island but never succeeded. In terms of our understanding of the past this is important because historians over the last three hundred years, the period Scotland has been linked to England in the United Kingdom, have primarily adopted a British outlook. This has meant a quite unbalanced tendency to study the Romans in Scotland, as if they were in any way as important to how Scotland developed as they were to England, and to a lesser extent, Wales. This, combined, I believe, with a deliberate and at times all-pervasive Christian bias, has meant that far little attention has been paid to what Scotland was like in pre-Christian times. It has led to some crazy ideas like the one that the Presbyterian church was preceded in matters of doctrine and rectitude by the Columban church itself! Before going any further into what I think we can discern of pre-Christian beliefs in early Scotland, I should say that I am not a pagan. I was raised as an atheist and retain a healthy scepticism towards anything mystical or supernatural. I will however accept the evidence of my own senses when dealing with ideas and experiences, and can say that I am no longer as much of a materialist as I was in my younger days.

Scotland developed differently from the rest of Britain for most of the first half of the 1st Millennium and in retaining its essentially tribal structure, was therefore much more likely to preserve those ideas and precepts that underpinned the Old Religion. Partially this was undoubtedly due to the physical difficulties of the country, particularly north of the Highland Line. History has in fact served Scotland ill. The needs of a British state, with many Scots regularly in prominent positions, has meant that the vast differences between the histories of England and Scotland have all too often been diminished where they have not been ignored. Periods such as that immediately after the Battle of Culloden, recently shown to have been a much more close-run thing than had previously been acknowledged, are never examined in detail precisely because they point up matters that work against the idea of Britishness. This is ironic for the very term Britain could well have originated up here in the north. Jean Markale, one-time Professor of Celtic Studies at the Sorbonne in Paris, suggested that the term Britain came from *Prydein* which in turn derived from *Pretani* which was the Welsh or P-Celtic equivalent of the Gaelic *Cruithne*, which was what the Irish and Scots Gaels called the Picts. Again this is not a matter of blame. Just as story in pre-literate times serves to educate the young and continue the culture of the community, so history has always been about preserving the cohesion of society. However history is the winners' version of events, while story can preserve some of the losers' take on what happened. It is also true to say that in the modern world we understand the role of, and perhaps the need for, revisionist history.

CHAPTER SEVEN

Landscape markers

Lack of Early Scottish manuscripts – Cailleach survives in story and place names – suggestion of a Fairy Cult – rituals at ancient sites – druids and shamans – nemetons – Cailleach and mountains – Paps and Ciochs – dual goddess – mountain clusters – Cailleach and Bride in the landscape – cauldron as symbol – Norse roaring cauldron

DUE TO THE ROMAN's inability to take control Scotland was spared many of the substantial changes that took place south of Hadrian's Wall and therefore it seems fair to assume that stronger links to earlier patterns of belief as well as social behaviour survived here. The brief appearance of the Romans however meant also that the tribespeople of Scotland were exposed to literacy much later than their southern cousins. This, combined with the destruction of so much early literature in Scotland means we do not have any Scottish material to compare with either *The Mabinogion* of the Welsh or the Early Irish Sagas that deal with the *Tuatha de Danaan*, *Cu Chulain* and *Finn MacCoul*. Scotland does however have a strong storytelling tradition which has never totally disappeared, in which, just as the Picts and Britons shared Arthur, the Gaelic-speaking Scots had the stories of *Finn MacCoul* and the *Fianna* in common with their fellow Q-Celtic-speaking cousins, the Irish. The fact that settlers from Ireland did not establish Dalriada at the beginning of the 6th century should not be taken to mean there were no cultural links between Scotland and Ireland. Just as the Picts were in contact with the Gododdin, the Britons of Strathclyde and the peoples further south, so the Scots of Dalriada were in regular contact with the tribes in Ireland. Even today many of us Scots are proud to claim Irish blood in our recent ancestry. However the idea of the Dalriadic plantation taking place around 500 CE has led to a ridiculous overestimation of Irish influence on Scotland. This again can be partially put down to the obsession with defining people by the language they speak. Some scholars have tired to trace everything that occurs in Scottish Gaelic tradition back to Irish influence. One of the most striking examples of this is that it has been said on many occasions that the *Cailleach Bheur*, the Hag of Winter in Scotland came to us from Ireland. As we shall see there is one particular instance of this that if it were not so wrong headed, would be hilarious but this general idea is unsustainable. As the great folklorist Katherine Briggs asked so many years ago, why if the Cailleach originated in Ireland then are there so many more Cailleach stories and place names in Scotland than Ireland?

The Cailleach occurs extensively in that great collection of Scottish story *Popular Tales of the West Highlands* by JF Campbell first published in 1860 and collected amongst the Gaelic speaking population of the Highlands and Islands. This is a lot later that *The Mabinogion* or Irish tales like the *Tain Bo Cualnge* were first written down but, as we have seen, story can retain information over remarkable lengths of time and perhaps Campbell's collections can help us get a better picture of some of the beliefs of the far past. Time after time the Cailleach occurs as a giant supernatural creature with whom various heroes battle, and she is always defeated and usually killed. This might well be due to the effect of the Christianisation of stories that predate the arrival of that religion. The Cailleach though was also a landscape maker. There were tales of her creating Loch Ness and Loch Awe, Ben Vaichard and Liitle Wyvis in Ross-shire, and she left her mark on a variety of notable Scottish mountains. Significantly she was also associated in traditional belief with the creation of weather, particularly bad weather and this is related to many of her place names in the landscape. The landscape is an area where, like story, the people of the past, our ancestors, have left what might well be clues to how they perceived the world.

We have seen that in Scotland there are a series of hills that have been the focus of a great deal of activity throughout history and before. These places like Traprain Law, Edinburgh, Stirling and Dumbarton Rocks with their Arthurian connections are perhaps also linked in ancient belief with a series of mountains in the Scottish landscapes. Each of these locales is linked to the aforementioned Nine Maidens motif. They are also associated in an ancient tale with Ben Nevis, the highest point in the British Isles. Here they are the Cailleach, the Winter Hag herself, and her eight sisters who ride out together to hammer frost into the land with their *slachadan* or magic hammers or wands. This ancient giant female occurs throughout the Scottish landscape in both the Gaelic and Scots speaking parts of the country and though at first sight she is the absolute antithesis of fertility and regeneration, we shall see that she is in fact intimately intertwined with such ideas.

In Perthshire in the centre of the country there is a mountain known as Schiehallion which has generally been translated as meaning The Fairy Hill of the Caledonians. Caledonian as we have seen, was one of the names the Romans consistently used to describe the native tribes of what was then Scotland, the other term being Pict. Belief in the fairies lasted late in Scotland, the Australian poet AD Hope going so far as to suggest an actual Fairy Cult being still in existence in the 16th century.[29] This suggestion is very interesting and whether or not one likes the term Fairy Cult he makes a strong case for ritual behaviour that seems to have had a very long history. No one has ever completely solved who, or what the fairies were, some people seeing them as supernatural creatures who were expelled from the Christian heaven for supporting Satan, others as folk memories of our ancestors, some as a long disappeared early race of people and others as elemental spirits. There are still people today who believe that such elemental creatures can be found here.

What is clear is that many traditions link fairies to specific sites and it is also true that many of these are locations which turn out be ancient monuments of one kind or another. There are many stories of people, usually musicians, being spirited away by the fairies. In these tales the musicians generally come out from these *sìdh* or fairy mounds, believing that they have been playing overnight but then find that they have been away for decades and sometimes as much as a hundred years. In many instances once they realise how much time has past they simply fade away like smoke, but there are instances where musicians are said to have flourished and become successful with the help of the fairies, or other supernatural creatures associated with such places. Usually however the recipient of such help breaks their luck by telling others the source of their fortune at which point they lose everything they had accrued through supernatural help. In both types of tale it is clear that the fairies were believed to be dangerous and similar types of stories survive in many other lands.

We have looked at the suggestion that stories of this type might actually be a memory of rituals that were carried out at chambered cairns and other sites of communal burial to honour the ancestors, and even to ask for their help at the end of Autumn to ensure that crops would grow the following Spring. We now know that the old notion of such major structures being the sites of the burial of important males is not sustainable and it is clear that in their construction and use that the chambered cairns, like the stone circles and other major monuments, were the product of communal activities that we would nowadays interpret as essentially religious, though sacred might be a better way of understanding this. By this I mean that we do not know how the beliefs leading to the ritual activities that took place at sites like chambered cairns and stone circles were structured. I have already mentioned the possibility that the Gods and Goddesses of both Germanic and Celtic mythologies might have been subjected to an organised presentation conforming to Classical models that did not reflect the actual belief of the pre-Christian peoples in both cultural areas. Recently many people have been interpreting the practices of the past in the light of what we know of modern shamanic practice and this might well be another example of imposing what we think we know, on what we are trying to understand. Shape-shifting has already been mentioned and it has been suggested by many commentators that the pre-Christian peoples of North-western Europe used psychedelic substances in their rituals. This is suggestive of what we know about modern shamans but we do not have sufficient data to say that the practitioners of ritual in pre-Christian times in the British Isles were shamans. Shamans generally exist within small communities, generally kin-groups but we should not allow similarities to lull us into believing that what is now must have been what was then. Until very recently the buzz word for pagan practitioners was druid, and this has been replaced, in many people's attempts to understand the past, by shaman. We cannot be sure.

What we can be sure of is that the ancient monuments that were the sites of ritual were raised by extensive communal action and given what we know of tribal societies these should be understood as being created by the community for itself, and not for some supposed elite individual or group. Within tribal structures the chief or other person of standing is part of the tribe, not separate from it and certainly not above it. As I have already suggested however there do seem to have been groups of religious practitioners who lived apart from the tribe at significant sites in the landscape. We will also see in material that survives in the landscape, recurrent themes that can tell us a lot of how our ancestors understood both that landscape and in many ways themselves. Mythology is an attempt to explain the world in understandable terms and the explanation of how the environment itself came into being is a fundamentally important part of this. There appears to be a link between the mounds of the fairies, the various prominent hills that have been mentioned and some of the mountains of Scotland. In his book *Highland Myths and Legends* my storytelling colleague George MacPherson tells a story of two young people making love in a stone circle while their community looked on. Such behaviour would be quite acceptable for people untainted by the idea of sin, and public lovemaking at specific scared times of the year has been attested in many societies. The idea of such behaviour it seems was to encourage fertility and regeneration in an often uncertain world. It makes sense that places that were created for rituals associated with such worship would be the focus for much human activity. There are a great many mounds around Scotland, and the fact that many Early Christian churches were built on raised mounds reinforces the idea that these were already sacred sites when the Christians arrived and implemented the policy of re-using 'pagan precincts'. Due to one of the many unfortunate misunderstandings that plague our understanding of Scotland's past, many mounds have been interpreted as mottes, or sites of Norman-French motte and bailey structures. While it is possible that some such mounds were re-used in this fashion, there were never enough Norman-French nobles here to account for the number of mounds. In an intriguing article Professor GWS Barrow looked at the place named *nemeton* in Scotland.[30] This term is thought to have signified oak-grove, and Barrow noticed several of these occurring in forms like *nemed*, *neimhidh* etc. Some of these are actual hills like Duneaves near Fortingall – where what is believed to be Europe's oldest living tree exists and which was the site of Beltain rites till modern times – Creag Neimhidh south west of Inverness and Tarnavie in Strathearn, which has a story of a 'wee man' coming out from inside the hill to remonstrate with a local man digging on the hill. Others like Neudosk in Strathdon and Rosneath with its *Tom A'Mhoid*, or the Court Hill, occur alongside mounds, while Finavon near Forfar has an association with Nine Maidens, whom we have seen were linked to many prominent and important hills. Navidale, just north of Helmsdale is the site of an early Christian church and a Pictish Symbol Stone found there had a cauldron symbol on it. It is now in Dunrobin Castle. The link between mounds and hills though tentative does appear to exist, along with other recurring motifs. And perhaps there is something in the name Ben Nevis, our highest mountain, with its own Cailleach tales that corresponds to this. Professor W. Nicolaisen suggested it possibly derived from a forgotten word like *nebh* meaning mist or cloud.[31] This in reference to a mountain matches quite well with the original meaning of Cailleach, the veiled or hooded one. Professor Nicolaisen also commented in conversation that it is close to the Germanic Nebel meaning mist or fog.

On Schiehallion there is a scar on the mountain known as *Sgriob na Caillich*, the scrape or drag of the Cailleach. This particular place name is duplicated on *Beinn an Oir* one of the three Paps of Jura in the Inner Hebrides. Here the *Sgriob,* a massive groove on the western slope of the mountain, is said to have been made by the Cailleach being pulled by a man called MacPhie who was escaping from her control. This is also the location, in another story, for the destruction of the Seven Big Women of Jura, who were possibly originally nine in number. The destruction of the

Seven Big Women of Jura occurs in the story of *Mac Iain Direach* in Campbell's *Popular Tales of the West Highlands* and like the destruction of the Cailleach in so many other instances in the same volumes, might well be a memory of the superseding of the old, essentially pagan religion, by Christianity. There are other notable peaks that have associations with the Cailleach, and her counterpart the Carlin, Cailleach being Gaelic and Carlin Scots, our other indigenous tongue.

We have seen that Ben Nevis, the highest mountain in the British Isles was associated with the Cailleach and her eight sister hags with their magic wands. Ben Nevis is part of the Mamore range of mountains, a term which has been seen as deriving from *Mam,* the female breast.[32] *Cioch* and *Mam* are not the only terms for the female breast that we find in the Scottish landscape. There area whole series of Paps in the Scottish landscape, a term that means teat or nipple but can also refer to the whole female breast. The best known of these are probably the aforementioned Paps of Jura in the Inner Hebrides and the Paps of Fife, east and west Lomond Hill. There are others however and in Lothian the clearly breast shaped North Berwick Law and Arthur's Seat are known in local lore as the Paps of Lothian. There are various Maiden Paps, conical hills in the landscape and other linked names derive from the Gaelic for Pap, Cioch. These include Lochnagar on Deeside, originally Beinn na Ciochan and Bennachie in Aberdeenshire. Lochanagar has two relevant peaks Meikle and Little Pap and Bennachie's clear nipple shaped peak known nowadays as Mither Tap was in earlier times referred to as Mither Pap. The reference to Mither, Scots for Mother is telling. Tinto Hill which we looked at earlier, has its Pap Craig. If, as I suggest, the Cailleach who is the epitome of Winter in much traditional Scottish lore, was in her earliest form a Mother Goddess figure, this reference to the Breast of the Mother suggests something specific. If the belief was that the landscape was created by the Cailleach, or her counterpart in Scots, the Carlin, it is possible to surmise that breast shapes in the landscape were believed to have been put there by her to be noticed. It has already been noted that Dumbarton Rock from the south east forms the shape of a pair of female breasts, if not exactly symmetrical. It is also noteworthy that from Edinburgh Castle, with its own Arthurian connections from at least the time of the Gododdin, you can see the Paps of Fife, the Paps of Lothian, *Schiehallion* and *Ben Ledi*, the Hill of God which has its own *Cnoc a Cailleach* on the summit. Given that in pre-literate societies words like symbols can have layers of meaning it is noticeable that *cioch* could be seen as referring to the breast of a young woman, and *mam* as that of an older woman. This may in some way reflect the relationship between Bride, Goddess of Summer and the Cailleach, Hag of Winter. We should however expect the belief in such a powerful Mother Goddess to have survived elsewhere than in the mountains. One traditional explanation of the name Hebrides has been dismissed by linguists. It tells us that while she was making Scotland that the Cailleach dropped an apron full of stones thus creating the Hebrides, the Y Bride or Islands of Bride. If the duality of the Cailleach and Bride has any merit this idea should surely be given some credence.

We should now consider what Cailleach means. Although most commentators have been happy to translate the term in its oldest form as hag, it is also a term that has come to be used for a Christian nun. This is because the underlying meaning of the term is the veiled or hooded one. We know that Christianity made a habit of adopting extant religious sites, practices and stories so it should not be seen as surprising that the term for nun originally referred to what was obviously a Goddess. *Schiehallion* is a case in point for like other mountains such as Ben Nevis, Lochnagar on Deeside, the Paps of Jura and even the Paps of Fife, it is often wreathed in cloud. It is veiled. Weather changes occur when clouds gather first round the highest peak in an area and this makes absolute sense when linked to mountains or peaks that have an association with Mother Goddess figures. Two cases should serve to show this. We have seen that Lochnagar, the highest point of the South eastern Grampians has Meikle Pap and Little Pap, but it also has a stream called *Allt-na-cailleach* – as does Ben Nevis – and a further peak, not breast shaped, called *Casteal na Caillich*, the Cailleach's castle. It is also the site of a midsummer sunrise pilgrimage. Bennachie in Aberdeenshire not only has the nipple shaped peak called Mither Tap, it also has a Maiden causeway, A Shannoch Craig, which is a reference to the fires of Samhain or Halloween, and at its foot it has the famous Pictish Symbol Stone the Maiden Stone. Bennachie is associated in story and song with notable giants. This association with the Maiden is perhaps also significant for in one of the stories of Ben Nevis the Cailleach keeps Bride, the Goddess of Summer, imprisoned. It has been sometimes suggested Bride is her daughter but in reality would appear to be her alter ego. Bride escapes briefly at *Imbolc*, the beginning of February but is recaptured only to finally break free at *Beltain*, the great feast of the ancient peoples that provided with *Samhain* the two great turning points of the ancient Scottish year. This was not in any way restricted to Scotland, it is merely that by a series of historical accidents we know a great deal about such practices here.

These place names, historical monuments and stories all serve to suggest that prominent hills like Bennachie and Lochnagar had an important place in the psychological landscape of the prehistoric population. The point that story was located in the landscape of the audience to ensure maximum relevance further suggests that Lochnagar with its Cailleach place names and significant peaks, and Bennachie with its combination of place names, stories and historical monuments were particularly significant. The emphasis on the Cailleach, the Maiden and the female breast would there-fore have helped to make made these, in one way or another, sacred spaces. If the Cailleach or Carlin was said to have been the creator of the landscape then as I have said the occurrence of specific shapes redolent of the female body could only have been interpreted as deliberate. While this is incapable of absolute proof it does seem possible, even likely. The fact that at Bennachie the historical monuments like the Maiden Causeway and the Pictish Symbol Stone are separated by a considerable stretch of time shows that the place held its significance over a long period. Another telling fact is the simple fact that Mither Tap (Pap), and Meikle Pap are visible for considerable distances, even if in the case of the latter, one has to be on the hill-tops of Deeside to realise this. Their shape, their visibility and their regular invisibility due to be being veiled in cloud all reinforce them as places associated with the Cailleach. To return briefly to Schiehallion, it is clearly visible from both Arthur's Seat and Calton Hill in Edinburgh, particularly when it is snow covered in winter, the time of the Cailleach. This is a distance of over 60 miles. We should consider the possibility that when the Romans referred to the peoples of Scotland as the Caledonians they were describing a collection of tribes or peoples whose understanding of the world was shaped by common beliefs.

The Cailleach and Bride in their respective associations with winter and summer, are opposite poles of the year and there are several instances where tradition tells us that the Cailleach turns into Bride on Beltain morning. In Scots tradition the same polarity can be seen in the landscape where we have the Carlin and the Maiden. The Paps of Fife, are East and West Lomond Hill and close to West Lomond Hill till relatively recently there was a stone pillar, that looked human and was referred to as Carlin Maggie, supposedly a witch turned to stone by the Devil. Nearby there is a natural perpendicular hole through rock called the Maiden Bore which was crawled through by women in a fertility rite. This type of polarity where place names refer to the crone and the young woman are found elsewhere. On Ben Ledi, usually translated as the Hill of God, in the Trossachs, the alternative name of the hill is still attached to an outcrop of rock close to the summit, *Cnoc a Cailleach* – *Cnoc* means outcrop. Directly below it in Glen Lubnaig is a chapel dedicated to St Bride, a Christianised version of the earlier goddess figure Bride. Here it is necessary to stress that Bride in Scotland is not an imported version of the Irish Bride or Bridget but an indigenous figure. In Scotland she is associated in Gaelic tradition with adders, and Ireland famously has no snakes, and there are also references to traditions stating she is buried in Scotland.[33] She would appear to have been common to much of these islands for these is little doubt that the Brigantes of northern England in Roman times also worshipped her. On the slopes of Goat Fell on Arran, part of the so-called Sleeping Warrior, we find the *Ceum na Caillich* directly opposite *Cioch na h-Oighe*, or pap of the young maiden at the head of Glen Sannox. Elsewhere we find the Cailleach and Bride at opposite ends of Craigshouse Bay on Jura as another instance of this recurring polarity. The Carlin in Scots tradition is also a landscape maker and in one notable Middle Scots poem she is said to have 'lut [let] fart North Berwick Law', itself a prominent pap shape in the landscape, known as one of the Paps of Lothian and the focus of extensive witchcraft activity in the time of James VI.

The recurrence of linked place names referring to old and young women along with the Pap names themselves support the idea of a belief system in which the Mother Goddess was manifest in a recurring duality. The hoard of iron ware found as votive offerings in Carlingwark Loch near the Border with England is probably another instance of this type of belief and it is notable that amongst the hoard were several cauldrons. Cauldrons as we have seen have a specific set of meanings associated with fertility and renewal within British and Irish traditions and they continued to be linked in popular story with witchcraft long after Christianity was supposedly universal here. There are other cauldrons in both British and Norse sources that underpin the power and relevance of the symbol.

In early Welsh Literature there are references to the Thirteen Treasures of Wales which include *Pair Dyrnwch Gawr*, the Cauldron of Dyrnwch the Giant: if meat for a coward were put in it to boil, it would never boil; but if meat for a brave man were put in it, it would boil quickly, which is very like the Cauldron of the Dagda in Irish sources. A similar treasure is *Mwys Gwyddno Garanir*, the Hamper of Gwyddno Long-Shank. Food for one man would be put in it, and when it was opened, food for a hundred men would be found in it. This is the same character who found Taliesin in is basket after he had been cast adrift by Cerridwen. Mention has already been made of the links and similarities between 'Celtic' and Norse traditions and legends and there are many cauldrons that feature in Scandinavian and Germanic mythology. Jakob and Wilhelm Grimm, the brothers whose stories did so much to preserve ancient tales, wrote extensively on cauldrons in their classic work, *Teutonic Mythology* that analyses the mythology of the Germanic-speaking peoples in depth. They mention that cauldrons were sometimes used among the Cimbri, the tribe that inhabited Jutland, now part of modern Denmark, in Roman times, and specifically mentions priestesses tending such cauldrons. This is like the Nine Maidens around Cerridwen's cauldron and given that the earliest Norse mythology was written down by Christian monks it is at least possible that here we have a misinterpretation, deliberate or otherwise of the use of magical cauldrons to awaken the dead. He also tells us that trolds, a kind of elves, had copper kettles, and that the Norse god Thor seized a great cauldron from Hymir, leader of the Frost Giants which may echo the same idea as Arthur's attack on Annwn to capture a cauldron. Hymir and the cauldron come together in the story of *Hvergelmer*, the roaring cauldron, where the Frost Giants' bodies were ground down to create the physical world by, in some versions, Nine Maidens. We shall return to *Hverglemer*. Grimm also mentions traditions regarding brewing-kettles or cauldrons, linking them with witch-craft. Another interesting cauldron exists in Frensham in Surrey, England. It is called Mother Ludlam's cauldron and local legend says it was gift from the fairies that was never returned. Here again we see the linking of a cauldron with the supernatural and the use of the term Mother is a recurring theme in traditions from all over England that concern witches or wise women. The term mother is a clear reference to some sort of nurturing or perhaps instructive role and might well preserve a link back to a time when belief in the Mother Goddess was effectively universal. The Cailleach's link to both cauldrons and the figure of Bride, who is fertility and regeneration personified, strongly support the idea she too was once a mother goddess figure. There are hundreds of Cailleach place names in the Scottish landscape and, as at Craigshouse Bay on Jura, they are not all on high mountains.

CHAPTER EIGHT

The Feminine Principle

*Calanais and cailich na mointich – lunar standstill –
Cailiness cluster – Glen Clova – Sleeping Giant of Benarty –
Beltain rites – continuities and survivals – Celtic studies
ignoring Scotland – Islands of Women – possibility of
deer-priestesses – Pictish symbols – Thomas the Rhymer*

ONE OF THE MOST striking instances of the Cailleach in the land-scape occurs on the island of Lewis in the Outer Hebrides. On the western edge of Lewis overlooking Loch Roag lies the megalithic complex of Calanais with the well known Celtic cross shaped complex of standing stones at its heart. It is nowadays believed that Calanais was set up to watch the occurrence every 16.8 years of the lunar standstill. This is when the moon rises on consecutive nights at the most westerly point of its travels across the sky. Suggestions have been made that when the Roman geographer Strabo mentioned the god Apollo dancing every nineteen years at the winged-temple in Hyperborea, he was referring to Calanais. Hyperborea, the Land beyond the North Wind, is believed to refer to the British Isles. As we know, the megalithic builders who raised Calanais were part of a cultural milieu that encompassed all of the north-eastern littoral of the Atlantic Ocean and at least some of the Mediterranean area so there is no reason to doubt that Mediterranean people could have been aware of such a far-off place. I write this in a year, 2006 when the lunar standstill takes place, and many people will be going to Calanais to observe the phenomenon. It will in fact happen several times this year and according to archaeo-astronomer Doug Scott, an equally good, if not better view of the standstill can be had from the stone setting at Nether Largie near Kilmartin in Argyll, close to other significant locales.

At Calanais the main avenue of standing stones is aligned to observe the standstill and the moon itself appears to skip along a line of low hills to the south. This line of hills makes an outline of a female figure which is known locally as *Cailich na Mointich*, the Old Woman of the Moors. The effort put into the erection of the main stone circle and the more than twenty other megalithic structures and alignments in the immediate area, show considerable effort, and the link to a Cailleach figure here can hardly be coincidental. Possibly as late as the 19th century there were local people who had the hereditary role of raising the neid-fire at the stones on Beltain. On several occasions I have been assured by Gaelic language specialists that there can be no possible link between the name *Calanais* and the term *Cailleach*, the different spellings of a single and a double 'l' reflecting the totally different pronunciations, and thus meanings. Given the link between the stone circle and the *Cailich na mointich* this seems an overly negative statement, particularly if, as I suggest in this book we are dealing with a goddess figure who seems to have been known to the people who built the megaliths over five thousand years ago, and was still extant, if in a diminished form, in traditional tales collected in the 19th century.

I am unaware that anyone has as yet come up with a generally accepted interpretation of the term *Calanais* though most people have accepted that the second part reflects the Germanic term ness, point of land.

Far to the south on the Rhinns of Galloway, where the Welsh Triads claimed Arthur had one of his forts, there is a similar name. It is Cailiness Point, a peninsula overlooking Luce Bay. On the peninsula behind the point itself or close by there are the following; a supposed 'motte', the place name Kirkmaiden, some standing stones and traces of more than one stone circle. There is also a St Bride's Well, traditions of another 'Lady Well' and several Early Christian Churches. There is also a suggestion that Kirkmaiden refers to St Medana, one of the variants of Monenna, who was an Early Christian Saint said to have been accompanied by Nine Maidens.[34]

The area is rich in archaeological finds showing it has been in constant human occupation since the Stone Age, hardly surprising considering both its fertility and coastal location. However the clustering of links to the Old Religion makes a compelling comparison with *Calanais*, not that far away in terms of the sea travel that we now know has been regular since megalithic times. St Modwenna whose name is an accepted variant on Monenna, was said to have been baptised in a pool of abundance which again is suggestive of the cauldron of fertility. Time and again we find various combinations involving early Christian figures, mounds, the Hag, the Maiden, ancient monuments and cauldrons which echo the association between the Cailleach and significantly shaped mountains, ancient monuments and cauldrons. Calanais itself has various traditions involving such resonant concepts as a supernatural cow giving milk in time of famine and tales of witches.

There are other reclining figures in the Scottish landscape. The best known is probably the Sleeping Warrior on the island of Arran and there is said to be a female figure in the landscape at Ben Cruachan. Along the lines of *Agaidh Artiair* there is a face in hills on the southern side of Glen Clova in Angus. This has Glen Cally, possibly derived from Cailleach, immediately behind it and a cluster of place names relating to females at its foot including a Bride reference. Clova, like Clyde is probably derived from an ancient local goddess name.

In Fife there is the Sleeping Giant of Benartey, a name that some people have suggested refers to Arthur. Benartey has a cluster of interesting place names around it including Navitie Hill, a nemeton name and Gruoch's Well, said to have been named for Macbeth's wife Gruoch but possibly related to an ancient supernatural being the Gruagach, associated in some folk tales with libations poured into cup-and-ring marks. To my eyes this reclining figure on the south side of Loch Leven is female.

A considerable proportion of the sites we have mentioned have been associated with significant rituals in the past. Schiehallion, visible from over 60 miles away in clear weather is a case in point. Like Bennachie with its Shannoch Craig, Tinto Hill and many other sites, people came here on important days in the pre-Christian calendar. Early reports we have from Schiehallion mention a well on the west side of the mountain where young people from the surrounding area gathered on the morning of the first of May, the ancient feast of Beltain. Many such customs were remnants of earlier sacred rituals which involved whole communities and in the act of drinking from such a well or washing their faces in it, these young people were preserving a continuity that might well stretch back thousands of years. The fact that Schiehallion's summit can be seen from as far away as Edinburgh's Calton Hill, the site of the modern Beltain, raises the possibility that many of these ancient sacred mountains blazed simultaneously with bonfires on Beltain, Samhian and perhaps other notable days like Midsummer, still a time of pilgrimage on Lochangar. As late as 1840 an observer noted at least 30 Shannoch or Samhain fires on hilltops between Dunkeld and Aberfeldy in Perthshire, a distance of roughly eighteen miles. That so many of these major mountains are in line of sight with each other suggests that there was more than a local awareness to many of these rituals, strengthening the case for some sort of shared or communal view of the goddess in the landscape.

More localised version of these fire-hills were widespread and some can be seen in place names like *Tom-nan-ainneal*, small hill of the fire, at Killin, *Cnoc-nan-ainneal*, knoll of the fire on Iona, itself a scared place before the arrival of Columba, and in Scots speaking areas, Tarbolton in Ayrshire, from *Tor Bealltain*, Beltain-hill and Needs Law close to the border with England south of Hawick. Here the name derives from *neid*-fire, an old term for the fires that were kindled at Beltain. These fires had to be raised by friction, using fire drills which were in some cases so big that they required nine men at a time to turn them. The term *neid* has been the subject of much speculation and given that one of the customs at Beltain was to drive the cattle between two fires, it is tempting to see some connection with the Scots word *neat*, meaning cattle. These fires have been described in some sources as being made up of nine sacred woods, one of which was juniper. Its pungent smoke is known to have antiseptic qualities so yet again we may be seeing an ancient widespread ritual carried out at a sacred feast which had an eminently practical function. Some of the Beltain fires were lit into the 19th century though the people involved, generally young unmarried folk, were having fun, rather than deliberately perpetuating ancient ritual practices. Languages and even beliefs had changed but people were still carrying out rituals that had been performed by their distant ancestors. While the original religious concepts behind widespread activities at or around Beltain may have been long gone, it is noticeable in many instances that, possibly because the participants were mostly young unmarried people, there was always some level of sexuality involved.

Doug Scott the archaeo-astronomer has recently told me that several Pictish Symbol Stones – the stones at Aberlemno are a case in point – seem to preserve important alignments from the Bronze Age and possibly the Stone Age.[35] The Aberlemno roadside stones – there is a major Pictish stone in the nearby kirkyard depicting the Battle of Dunnichen in 685 – are close to the kirk, or church, in Aberlemno. This clearly reinforces the idea of Christian re-use of sites that in some cases had been in sacral use for thousands of years. While we cannot be sure that this meant the Picts, thought the about the landscape and who created it, in the same way as people in the Stone Age it does mean that, given the tenacity of the oral tradition, the possibility must exist that some ideas survived. This could be why we have so many Cailleach, Carlin, Bride and Maiden names in the landscape. As long as tales of these females were told, the names held on to some level of meaning. The names in the landscape helped to place the stories of these supernatural females for the storyteller's audience, and perhaps the names being in everyday use, helped some of the ideas and rituals that underpinned the Old Religion to survive. Such survivals can perhaps be seen in the figures and motifs that occur in the stories collected in Campbell's *Popular Tales of the West Highlands*. The storytellers were Christians but their tales preserve elements of traditions that went back to long before the advent of that religion in Scotland or Britain.

We have looked at the fact that Scotland was never subjected to any extended influence from Roman culture in the pre-Christian period and that the Normans who dominated so much of England and Wales were much less intrusive here. This means that the possibility of survival of old ways was stronger here. Even before Christianity became tolerated in England under the Romans, the various Roman troops, from such divergent areas as Friesland and Morocco, must have brought their own beliefs with them. This combined with the altering of traditional patterns of living, urbanisation and exposure to literacy within the area delimited by Hadrian's Wall must have meant some change to patterns of belief amongst the people. While Scotland must have been more conservative in religious terms because of the lack of Roman influence and the later arrival of Christianity, this has strangely not been the subject of much academic study. I have already made clear that I believe the term Celtic to be of little use in helping us to understand the far past in Scotland or even Britain but a point must be made about Celtic Studies. As an example of the problem we should consider three texts which until recently were core texts in the subject of Celtic Studies. These undoubtedly interesting and useful books are *Pagan Celtic Britain* by Anne Ross, *Celtic Heritage* by Alwyn and Brinley Rees and *The Celtic Realms* by Myles Dillon and Nora Chadwick. What is immediately obvious about these three books is that they have very few references to Scotland. Scotland, where a Celtic-speaking warrior society continued into existence until the middle of the 18th century, is effectively ignored, the authors preferring to rely on Early Medieval manuscripts from Ireland and Wales where such societies had already died out. They even make the point that the texts to which they refer are often preserving memories rather than experiences of the 'heroic' societies they represent. The possibility that tales collected in Scotland only a century and a half ago might be able to tell us about similar beliefs and relevant events is not considered. Could such stories, collected not much more than a century after the final collapse of a Celtic-speaking tribal society tell us anything about the far past. This idea is not fanciful. In Australia, Dreamtime tales of giant marsupials were dismissed as fantasy until fossilised bones of such creatures began to be found during mining for bauxite. Some of these were dated from forty thousand years ago and even more tellingly, were close to what were clearly cooking fires. With no written records the Aboriginal peoples passed on these stories for an incredible period of time. Other stories of landscape events like volcanic eruptions in specific places have since been discovered to be accurate.[36] What the aboriginal peoples of Australia did have was a symbolic language that they use to this day in their paintings. Some of these symbols have been used to help both remember and tell stories. The Pictish symbols might likewise have formed a symbolic language allowing the symbol Stones to be used in the storytelling process. The later Christian Cross-slabs with their depictions of Biblical scenes might have well been used in a similar fashion. Given that some of the Pictish Symbol Stones were clearly in use from a much earlier period, the symbols themselves might have been of great age before they were carved on the stones.

Apart from traditional stories there are also travellers' tales written about Highland society in the 17th and early 18th centuries which describe a type of society long disappeared elsewhere. Of course in Scotland it is impossible to ignore the reality that 'Celtic' society such as flourished under the Lordship of the Isles was heavily interpenetrated by Germanic influences. So too was Irish society in the latter years of the 1st Millennnium when the Vikings founded most of the modern cities of that island.

Apart from the rather strange anomaly of Scotland not being seen as worthy of study as a 'Celtic' society this raises a second point. As a result of there having been much less study of the literature of the Scottish Celtic-speaking populations, even though we do not have such early documentary evidence as in Ireland and Wales, the possibility must exist that things have been missed. Earlier I drew attention to Sjoestedt's contention that the Celtic and Norse mythologies had most likely been re-jigged to fit onto the pre-conceived and Classically driven assumptions of the monks who first wrote them down. This has not happened in Scotland. In fact there has been no attempt up to now to suggest a separate mythology for Scotland. Most commentators have been happy to suggest that the Gaels of Scotland must have had some mythological construct akin to the Irish. Those parts of Scotland in the far north that were part of Norway till the 15th century, retain some tales that are clearly Scandinavian in origin but no one has thought to suggest there was a Germanic type mythology here either. While we do have stories of Finn MacCoul in the west of Scotland that occur in Ireland, there are extremely few references to any of the *Tuatha de Danaan*, the Irish pantheon of gods, or of *Cu Chullain. Cu Chulain* the great heroic figure of the Ulster sagas was said in an Early Irish story, *The Wooing of Emer*, to have come to Scotland to be trained by *Scathach*, does not feature much either. *Scathach* incidentally gives *Cu Chulain* his arms in which echoes several instances in *The Mabinogion* where women give heroes arms. In many reference works on matters 'Celtic,' *Scathach*, a great female warrior, is said to have been based on Skye but the original tale has her living on an island on the east coast of Scotland.[37] There are very few islands off Scotland's east coast but one we have already mentioned might fit the bill – the Isle of May in the Forth estuary. This I have already mentioned as a possible site of Avalon, and here we have another mythical figure connected with the island.

The idea of the Island of Woman, which crops up in such diverse works as the *Life or Merlin* and the *Voyage of Bran* is not in any way restricted to the Celtic-speaking world and appears to be virtually universal. Nevertheless there are several instances of Islands of Women in Scottish lore, some involving Nine Maidens and, with the presence of the Cailleach and the Seven Big Women already mentioned, the island of Jura should perhaps be seen as one of these. I have suggested that these Islands of Women which occur in many societies throughout the world might be a memory of groups of priestesses living apart from the rest of society and the best known instance is probably the Isle of Druidesses off the Brittany coast. Here Pomponius Mela, writing in the 1st century, said there were nine weather-working, shape-shifting women in residence who were both healers and prophetesses.

The tribal peoples of Scotland must have had some sort of mythology and it is possible that such a mythology was located in the landscape, that it was common not just among the P-Celtic speakers but included the Q-Celtic speakers too. If the idea that Celtic and Norse mythologies were subjected to being re-organised to fit a structured and perhaps overly masculine model is accepted, we should re-consider what we think we know about pre-Christian religion in the British Isles. For the past couple of centuries there has been a great focus on Druids, to the extent that there are now latter day Druids in existence. Information regarding Druids is in fact pretty sparse, particularly in Scotland and many ancient sites appear to have stronger associations with females, either singly or in groups. I would go so far as to say there is more evidence for female religious practitioners of the Old Religion than male ones, and I have gone into this in depth in *The Quest for The Nine Maidens*. One of the early Gaelic examples of a Druid is *Fir Doirch* in the story of Finn and Sadv, the mother of Ossian. Finn rescues Sadv from *Fir Droich's* spell which had kept her in the form of a deer, and she then conceives Ossian. Before Finn's son is born, Sadv once again falls under the power of the Druid and disappears. Late, rout hunting, Finn finds his son who had been raised till then by his mother in the shape of a hind in cave high in the hills. Finn gives the boy the name *Oisin*, otherwise Ossian, meaning fawn. Finn's original name was *Demne* which has been interpreted as meaning small deer. The reference to *Sadv* taking on a hind's shape is reminiscent of the story of The Widow's Son in *Popular Tales of the West Highlands*. Here the hero is sent out to guard crops against a marauding hind. In an obviously late version of the tale, when the deer arrives he points his gun at her. However as he sights along the barrel he sees the deer as having a woman's head. He lowers the gun and sees only a deer. Raising the gun again, this time he sees a woman to the waist, and again lowers the weapon. In front of him again he sees only a deer and for a third time he raise the gun. This time he sees the complete form of a woman before him and when he lowers the weapon she retains her human form. He has broken the spell she was under. It seems to me that this might be a possible description of an actual deer priestess, taking off a deer costume. The existence of deer-priestesses and a Deer-goddess was suggested in the 1930s.[38] This might account for the mask type deer head on the Glamis Manse stone, something which also occurs on other Symbol Stones. We have seen that deer were closely associated with the Cailleach and in at least two of the Grail Romances *Erec et Enide* and the *Quete du Sant Graal* there are hunts for magical white deer, in the latter case the white deer changed into a man in front of the Grail heroes Perceval, Galahad and Bohort. Here again we see what may be faint memories of ancient pagan ideas surfacing in the medieval romances.

Be that as it may, an idea being currently considered amongst Scandinavian folklorists is that the probable ordering of early north-western European mythology along Classical lines has had one particular effect. It has been suggested that the influence of the combination of Classical and Christian ideas has meant that the mythological sources of the Germanic-speaking peoples of Scandinavia have been over-masculinised, i.e. that the role of the female figures was in fact much more important than has been recognised to date. The same could in all likelihood be said of the Celtic pantheon. Scotland has not been granted the privilege by scholars of having had its own mythology. Here I am suggesting that there was an indigenous mythology, and that mythology revolved around the linked figures of the Cailleach and Bride who survived in the parallel Scots (Germanic) tradition as The Carlin and the Maiden. It is possible that such an idea is truly ancient. Earlier I have mentioned that there appears to be a painting of Nine Maidens, who are closely associated with both the Cailleach and Bride, in the cave at el Cogul in Catalonia which is over 15,000 years old. It is impossible to verify that the concept of the Nine Maidens is this old or that their association with powerful Mother Goddess figures predates this, but it is certainly not impossible, and in fact I would suggest is quite likely.

The ancient calendar year was divided in two and in Scotland these seasons were the Time of the Big Sun, from Beltain to Samhain, and the Time of the Little Sun, from Samhain to Beltain. I should say that it is possible that the Time of the Little Sun was from Samhain to Imbolc, the 1st of February, the period when the nights are at their longest. The reason for suggesting this is that Imbolc is traditionally associated with Bride, it being the time of year when the first lambs began to be born, a sure sign of impending Spring. The great feasts of Beltain and Samhain are also linked with activities at many of the sites we have been considering and it is also well established that central communal activities took place at these times. In the Highlands and peripheral areas Beltain was the time that cattle were taken off to the sheilings, rough houses built specifically in the Highland pastures where the cattle, particularly the new-born calves, could grow fat over the summer. The reliance on cattle for meat, milk, leather and horn was central to the Highland tribes and like pastoral societies in many parts of the world their cattle were of supreme importance. They were also the main form of moveable wealth, and status was generally judged by how many cattle an individual, a family or a clan owned. This was why the role of cattle-raiding was so central to the role of the warriors in the clan or tribe, again conforming to what we know of similar societies in other areas and at different times. It is worth noting that deer were sometimes referred to as the Cailleach's cattle.

There are stories of hunters placating Cailleach before hunting for deer and there is an odd tale said to have been a true event that happened in 1773. Two hunters, searching for deer found themselves adrift on the Lochnagar massif in a snowstorm and met up with a strange and clearly supernatural woman on the plateau who saved their lives.[39] In mentioning the Glamis Manse stones earlier I drew attention to what I suggested was deer mask as well as the cauldron. The reason for suggesting this is that the Picts were expert at depicting animals. If this was a simple severed head it would look like one. In fact there are two curled appendages at the neck of the deer head which led me to think that it is a deer mask. Another Symbol Stone from Dunachton near Loch Insh in Strathspey, looks even more mask-like with what appears to be slit up the neck to allow it to be pulled over the head while on Meigle No1, there is yet another, akin to the one on the Glamis Manse stone. Another deer head on Monifeith No 2 has no additions and could be a severed deer's head, but it could also be a mask. The idea of the deer being symbolic of ancient beliefs finds an echo in the story of Thomas the Rhymer. Believed to have been a real person, Thomas of Ercildoune (Earlston) lived in the 13th century and it was said he went off to the land of Fairie for seven years. After returning and becoming a famous seer and visionary he was summoned back by the Queen of Faerie by two deer who came to his village to fetch him. He is strongly linked in tradition with the Eildon Hills which we have talked of before. The Queen of the Fairies and her use of deer in this instance cannot help but remind us of the Cailleach or the Carlin who is elsewhere known as the Queen of the Witches.

Intriguingly the Glamis Manse stone with the cauldron and deer head on what is generally accepted as the Christian side, has an adder and a salmon on the other, pagan side. The adder being the only indigenous Scottish snake, must be the serpent associated with St Bride in several ancient prayers in that great collection of

Gaelic prayers and sayings the *Carmina Gadelica*. The salmon is a symbol of knowledge and in an ancient Gaelic tale is said to live in a well fed by nuts falling from nine hazel trees surrounding it. These are the fruits of knowledge which give the salmon its powers. The hazel was one of the nine holy woods mentioned as being used in Beltain fires and in Scotland, there are several Calton Hills from *calldain*, hazel, including the one in Edinburgh where the revived Beltain rites now take place.

CHAPTER NINE

Into the Cauldron

*Beltain rite – Cailleach and the whirlpool – Dalriada and
Kilmartin – spirals and cup-and-ring marks – local tales –
Paps of Jura – Gododdin and Taliesin poem Harrying
of Annwn – Megalithic contacts – Hamlet's Mill – extensive
sea-travel since prehistoric times – Corryvreckan as
Charybdis – Conclusion*

WE HAVE SEEN HOW the traditions of Britain provided the motif
of the cauldron of abundance in the development of the Grail. In
Scotland despite the lack of early written sources we have seen
that many of the ideas that are central to what is often referred
to as Celtic culture were not only deeply rooted but extremely
long-lived. Even today we see the remnants of aspects of the Old
Religion in the widespread place names and tales of the Cailleach
and the Carlin. The tenacity of beliefs in these ancient figures can
be seen in a ritual that takes place around Beltain every year in
the Highlands of Perthshire. There at the foot of Glen Cailleach
at the head of Glen Lyon there is a structure, known as *Tigh na
Cailliche*, the House of the Cailleach. The house is in fact a kind of
shrine, built like a miniature version of the traditional Highland
Black House. Each May three curiously shaped stones, the
Cailleach herself, the Bodach, Old Man and the Nighean, Maiden
or daughter, are taken from the shrine and placed outside. The
shrine is then re-thatched with heather and the stones are left outside till Samhain. The house has also been referred to as *Tigh nam
Bodach* and the oldest meaning of Bodach relates to *bod*, penis.

This refers to a concurrent duality to that of the Cailleach and Bride, where we have the Cailleach and the Bodach. Just as pre-literate symbols can have layers of meaning so relationships between mythological figures can exist alongside each other, one meaning does not preclude another. *Tigh na Cailliche* has been the scene of this ritual for longer than anyone knows, though recently with the retirement of the shepherd on the local estate who had been tending the shrine, the continuity seemed likely to be broken. Thankfully someone else was found locally to take over the ritual. It seems the Cailleach has not yet disappeared totally. We have seen the remnants of what seems to have been the Old Religion abound in Scotland in place names and traditional tales and in the significantly shaped mounds, hills and mountains to which I have referred.

Nowadays we inhabit the landscape differently from our ancestors. Most of us live in cities or towns and when we travel our feet rarely touch the ground. We are generally in cars, trains and planes and even when we walk it is mainly on pavements. This is surely one of the reasons so many people flock to the hills in Scotland at every opportunity, to reconnect with our planet. But, just as we can still see the Paps that retain traces of how things once were, there are other surviving realities in the landscape of Scotland.

The most striking of these combines the ideas of the Cailleach and the cauldron in what is truly one of the wonders of the world. This is The Corryvreckan Whirlpool between the Hebridean islands of Jura and Scarba that spirals continuously whenever the Atlantic tide is running. One of only seven major whirlpools on our planet The Corryvreckan is an awesome sight. It is caused by the waters of the Atlantic Ocean coming round the south of Jura and north of Scarba and being forced back out through the Gulf of Corryvreckan. The waters are forced past a great underwater spike off the southern coast of Scarba and whirlpools form round it and rise to the surface. The spirals of water surge to the surface of the water breaking out in a great wave that sends a resounding boom off the cliffs of Scarba. The force of the waters coming through the Gulf of Corryvreckan then sends the clockwise spirals of the whirlpool into the oncoming Atlantic tide. After a while they are broken up by the power of the Atlantic, one of the most powerful geophysical forces on earth, by which time other spirals have been thrown up from the underwater spike.

That great underwater spike has a name, *An Cailleach* and to this day the whirlpools are known to Gaelic speakers in the western isles as *anail bhan-dia fo thuinne*, the breath of the goddess under the waves. The power of The Corryvreckan causes standing waves of water in the Gulf which can be as high as two or three metres, and the area has long been known as dangerous for shipping, particularly in the days before steam. I am constantly astounded that so few people in Scotland know of this wonder of the world on our doorstep but sailors of all kinds on the west coast, and all over the world, know of The Corryvreckan. How can such a magnificent geophysical event be so little known by the people of Scotland? We teach our children geography, increasingly there are classes devoted to environmental studies, yet still The Corryvreckan has remained known only to a few. The answer perhaps lies in the name of the underwater spike itself – *An Cailleach*. There are different tales as to how The Corryvreckan got its name and one of them, which is an obvious remnant of ancient mythology in its function of explaining the natural world, involves the Cailleach herself.

In this tale the Cailleach, the oldest being, the first born and in many tales the actual creator of the landscape, comes to the strait between Scarba and Jura at the beginning of winter to wash her Breacan, or plaid.[40] This was the traditional one-piece woollen garment of the Highlanders, men and women both. She was of course of gigantic stature, and after washing her plaid in the strait, she laid it out to dry over Ben Nevis and the Mamore Hills. Because she was the oldest being of all, her plaid was pure white, and this was the explanation given to children of the first snows of winter falling on the highest mountains in the British Isles. The story also refers directly to the phenomenon that takes place when the tides are at their highest and the weather at its worst as Winter, the Season of the Cailleach, comes on. The combination of high tides and gale force winds drive the seas into a fury and the spirals surge ever stronger until a great cauldron is formed in the waters between Scarba and Jura. Some reports say it forms a cauldron a hundred yards across and as much as thirty yards deep. Few people nowadays have seen this phenomenon as Scarba and the north coast of Jura are uninhabited and nobody would be daft enough to go out into those waters during a storm. To date all film of The Corryvreckan is of when it is running gently, though it is still dangerous. However the roaring noise it makes at its wildest can sometimes be heard over twenty miles away. Within living memory local sailors unfortunate enough to be out in one of these storms referred to 'the old woman trampling her blankets', a clear reference to the idea of the Cailleach washing her plaid.

If as I have suggested, the Cailleach was a central part of the Old Religion, it would only be sensible for the incoming religion of Christianity to try to diminish awareness of this dramatic geophysical event and its links to the old ways of thinking. There is a passing mention of The Corryvreckan in the *Life of Columba* written by a later Abbot of Iona, Adomnan, but the saint is said in a Life of St Ciaran to have been saved from the perils of the whirlpool by praying to St Bridget, who of course is just a Christian version of Bride. Some scholars commenting on this have said that it was a reference to a tidal race in the Aran Isles off the Irish coast and that The Corryvreckan Whirlpool was named after this place. The idea that a small tidal race can give its name to one of the most dynamic physical events that exist on the planet is just one more instance of the unfortunate distortion of Scotland's past due to the idea that Dalriada, the land of the Scots, was an Irish colony. Columba was the most important individual in the Christianising of Scotland and he was certainly Irish and too much has been made of this. One aspect of the emphasis on Irish connections has been the fact that it is only in the last half century that attention has begun to be paid to the fact that the Picts, Gododdin, and the Britons of Strathclyde were all P-Celtic speakers, unlike the Irish and Scottish Gaels who both spoke Q-Celtic languages. It also helps to account for the ongoing resistance to the idea that the Arthurian tales found in Scotland could be in any way genuine.

The heartland of the Scots, Dalriada, was centred around the Kilmartin valley at the head of the great peninsula of the Mull of Kintyre. The capital sat on the hill of Dunadd, a prominent peak in a flat landscape. From here looking west out over the flat lands of the Kilmartin one sees Jura and Scarba, over the waters of *An Dorus Mor*, the Great Door. The Scots of Dalriada were great sailors and there is no doubt they all knew about The Corryvreckan, its dangers and they surely remembered its mythic origins long after the Christian monks were singing their prayers.

Watching The Corryvreckan from above or from sea level is truly awe-inspiring. Its mythological importance is centred on its geophysical significance but this was not necessarily limited to the British Isles. In many places in Europe there are Stone Age and later carvings that utilise the spiral, a particularly beautiful set of them being at New Grange to the north of Dublin, and these spirals have often been interpreted as a symbol of the Mother Goddess. The Corryvreckan creates such spirals sixteen hours of every day, seven days of every week, fifty-two weeks of every year. It is possible that the cup-and-ring markings on the Stone Age rock carvings that are scattered all over Scotland might also have some link to The Corryvreckan. On the nearby Craignish peninsula there are several sets of these and the Kilmartin valley is a noted centre of such artefacts. This is not to suggest that cup-and-ring marks refer solely to The Corryvreckan, only that in their symbology there could be something that ancient peoples linked with the whirlpool. Kilmartin is a place where there are stone circles, standing stones and other ancient monuments like chambered cairns. Earlier I mentioned the stone circle at Nether Largie, is part of an alignment which Doug Scott believes might be of more significance even than Calanais or Stonehenge. The Kilmartin valley overlooking the waters leading into The Corryvreckan has long been considered one of the most sacred landscapes in Britain. Proximity to what might have been the most significant site associated with the ancient Mother Goddess could help account for this.

There are other stories about The Corryvreckan, one, clearly later, associates it with a Norse prince Breacan who failed the test of anchoring his ship there for three nights due to the 'frailty of a maiden' who had claimed to be a virgin and wasn't. This is a clearly post-Christian story with its inherent reference to sex as a sin, and was perhaps an attempt to replace the story of the Cailleach with something more suitable for good Christian ears. Another pair of local tales suggests the same process. There is a tradition that a sow swam out of The Corryvreckan and, landing on the Craignish peninsula, gave birth to nine piglets. These piglets grew up to give birth to all the boars in Scotland. In Loch Craignish there is a tiny island called *Dun na Nighean*, and it is perhaps stretching a point to suggest an association between these piglets and the island and that it is therefore a possible Nine Maidens site. The sow however is a well known symbol of the Mother Goddess in north western Europe.[41] This particular story is echoed by another later one. This one tells that Columba had come to the area in a time of famine. A local woman, not explicitly a witch, had somehow acquired nine piglets. Hearing that the saint was dispensing food to the local population, she hid her piglets in a wooden kist, or chest, and went to beg for food. The saint saw through her subterfuge and turned her away. She disguised herself and came back. Again she was turned away and disguised herself in another fashion. This time when she went to the saint he told her to go home and see what her actions had brought about. Filled with foreboding she ran home. There she opened the kist to see the piglets had all been turned into rats, which jumped out and scattered to give birth to all the rats in Scotland. This would appear to be a clear case of a Christian re-writing of an earlier pagan motif.

Previously I have mentioned the association of the Cailleach with deer and the name Jura, the island on the southern side of the whirlpool, comes from the Norse for Deer Island. It is also home to the Paps of Jura with their Cailleach and the Seven Big Women of Jura. The story that refers to the Seven Big Women *Mac Iain Direach* is one of many West Highland tales that also include the *glaibh soluis*, the sword of light, which is often sought for by heroes.[42] This is reminiscent of the idea of Arthur's supernatural sword Excalibur. Jura and Scarba are both full of deer, and stags regularly swim the Gulf of Corryvreckan at slack tide. At *Camus nam bearnach*, a flat area of land opposite the whirlpool on the south of Scarba there are the remains of a set of buildings. The Royal Commission on Ancient and Historic Monuments of Scotland makes the point that there is no ground nearby suitable for growing crops or raising animals and suggest that what stood here was some kind of settlement used seasonally for hunting sea birds.[43] Sea birds were long an important part of islander's diets but there is perhaps another explanation.

In the 19th century the German industrialist and amateur

archaeologist Heinrich Schliemann found the site of Troy by taking Homer's 'story' of the Iliad at face value – in the face of universal opposition from contemporary historians and archaeologists. The possibility exists that material in the oral tradition of Scotland might have similar value. If the *Gododdin* is accepted as referring to an actual historical event, the same might be true of other Welsh poems attested to both Aneurin and Taliesin, and to material that has come down through the Gaelic and Scots traditions. I have mentioned that Hugh MacArthur, Historian of the Clan Arthur had suggested that the *Priddeu Annwn*, the poem by Taliesin describing Arthur's raid on *Caer Sidi* to get a magic cauldron, might, along the lines of the accepted interpretation of the Gododdin poem, be a description of an actual event. He goes further and suggests that *Caer Sidi* was on Scarba and if there is any merit to the suggestion, the remains of buildings at *Camus nam bearnach* might well have been some kind of temple erected to house priests, or priestesses, beside what might well have been a very sacred location in the Old Religion. If it was seen to be so important and Arthur was, as suggested, on a Christian crusade, such a raid would make sense and poetic licence might well present The Corryvreckan as a magical cauldron.

The fact that Adomnan linked Columba to The Corryvreckan is indicative of something else. Of course Columba is likely to have passed The Corryvreckan sailing from Ireland to Iona but he was not the first. The megalithic builders knew this route three thousand years earlier and they too must have known of The Corryvreckan. Sailors always pass on knowledge of dangers to each other, and apart from any sacred significance it has, The Corryvreckan is still deadly for the unwary or the unprepared.

The Megalithic culture stretched from Morocco in the south, to Scandinavia in the north. Most commentators to date have suggested that the megalithic builders came to England, Ireland

and Scotland from the south. There is a traditional tale about the building of Calanais that says the stones were raised by black men who left after building them, leaving some priests behind. While this underlines the cultural range of Megalithic culture, we cannot be certain the influence always ran south to north. Cultural contact is a two way process and even if the first Megaliths were raised by incomers from the south they would be affected by what they found on their travels. And what could they have found on those travels more magnificent than the Corryvreckan Whirlpool?

Word of such a place, particularly as it seems to have been associated with the Mother Goddess, would have spread north and south along the Megalithic route, perhaps taking the idea of the spiral as a sacred symbol with it. The spiral of course occurs regularly nature but rarely in so dramatic a form as the whirlpool. In mythology the Mother Goddess generally had power over life and death, something that can be understood in the dual aspect of the Bride and Cailleach. Her own constant rebirth could be one of the fundamental ideas behind the idea of cauldrons of rebirth associated with her. This duality is also reflective of other aspects of life, night and day, Summer and Winter, male and female, up and down, positive and negative, young and old.

If my contention is correct, and The Corryvreckan is the most significant original idea behind the idea of cauldrons of rebirth and fertility, or poetry and inspiration, that arose in later tales and literature and that this went on to help form the concept of the grail, we would expect such a significant locale to be known well beyond the bounds of Scotland. We have seen there seems to have been attempts to disguise the importance of the whirlpool by associating it with the tidal race of the Aran Islands but this is perhaps not the only time such a transference has taken place.

The earliest version of the story of the Scandinavian story of

Hamlet, which derives from an older mythological figure Amlodhi was composed by Snaebjorn. He has been identified as one of the very first Vikings who sailed from Dublin to Iceland in the 9th century. His route is likely to have taken him past The Corryvreckan and it is inconceivable that the Viking raiders and settlers who came to the west of Scotland and Ireland did not know of it. In the poem Snaebjorn writes:

> Men say that the nine maidens of the island-mill are moving the hoist fierce mill of the skerries out beyond the outskirts of the earth, they who long ago ground Amlodhi's meal.[44]

This echoes a significant piece of Norse mythology in Hymir's Saga. Here, after being invited to a feast with the sea god Aegir, Thor goes to the Jotun, or Frost-Giant Hymir to get a huge cauldron in which to brew ale for the forthcoming feast. The upshot of this is a battle between the Gods of Asgard, the Aesir and the Frost giants led by Hymir, in which Thor and his companions were triumphant. There is perhaps an echo here of Arthur's raid to capture the cauldron in *Prideu Annwn*. Subsequently the bodies of Hymir and the rest of the Frost giants were ground down in the World-mill to create the physical world of humans. Mackenzie, in his *Teutonic Myth and Legend*, tells us the following:

> The great World-mill of the gods was under the care of Mundilfore. Nine giant maids turned it with much violence, and the grinding of the stones made such fearsome clamour that the loudest tempests could not be heard. The great mill is larger than is the whole world, for out of it the mould of the earth was ground. ...
>
> From Ymir's bones were made the rocks and the mountains; his teeth and jaws were broken asunder ... the giant maids flung the fragments hither and thither, and these are the pebbles and boulders. The ice-blood of the giant became the waters of the

vast engulfing sea. Nor did the giant maids cease their labours when the body of Ymir was completely ground. ... The body of giant after giant was laid upon the mill, which stands beneath the floor of the Ocean, and the flesh-grist is the sand which is ever washed up round the shores of the world. Where the waters are sucked thorough the whirling eye of the millstone is a fearsome maelstrom and the sea ebbs and flows as it is drawn down to Hvergelmer, 'the roaring cauldron', in Nifelheim and thrown forth again. The very heavens are made to swing by the great World-mill round Veraldar Nagli, 'the world spike', which is the Polar Star.[45]

It is interesting here that he mentions the World Spike as it is reminiscent of the physical spike that causes the whirlpool of The Corryvreckan. This idea of the World Spike or the Axis Mundi, is symbolically the centre of the world and/or the connection between Heaven and Earth and is known in virtually all cultures. It is sometimes seen as a link between the centre of the earth below our feet and the Pole Star in the skies above us and is thus linked to the understanding of the sequence of the equinoxes, the circling of the constellations in the sky above us. It takes over 25,000 years to complete one circuit of the precession of the equinoxes. It is the division of this period of time into twelve that gives us the signs of the Zodiac and the precession of the equinoxes has been understood for a long time. In *Hamlet's Mill*, subtitled *An Essay on Myth and the Frame of Time*, the authors say this about the World-Mill which they link to the precession:

Medieval writers ... located the gurgus mirabilis, the wondrous eddy, somewhere off the coast of Norway, or of Great Britain. It was the Maelstrom, plus probably a memory of the Pentland Firth.[46]

I would suggest that we do not have any reference to either the Maelstrom, the great whirlpool of the Lofoten Islands off the northern coast of Norway, or the Pentland Firth, but to The Corryvreckan itself. By the 8th century Norsemen were marauding regularly down through the Minch and the Irish Sea but their distant ancestors had sailed these waters as far back as Megalithic times. While the Maelstrom is one of the other major seven whirlpools, it seems unlikely to have been known either as early, or so widely as The Corryvreckan. It also does not have a spike, called after a goddess, at its heart. The Megalithic route, the trade routes for gold and amber between Britain and the Baltic and the Viking raiding paths all went south west from Norway. It wasn't until late in the 1st Millennium that Norseman started heading north westwards to Iceland and on to North America.

If the contention that the Old Religion centred round a female figure, the Mother Goddess, and writers like Marija Gimbutas have suggested this was the fact in mainland Europe in the third and fourth millennia BCE, then it is possible that the Cauldron of the Goddess was known over a wide area. In his book *Facing the Ocean,* Barry Cunliffe has shown the extent of trade and contact all over Europe thousands of years ago. This contact was generally by sea. To this day sailors swap stories and The Corryvreckan is still talked about by sailors. While the whirlpool is extremely dangerous it is also relatively accessible. Even in a sailing boat it is simple to get to either Scarba or Jura from the coast of Scotland, as long as one is aware of the tides and weather. People could have easily gone out to Scarba at slack tide to observe the whirlpool. Alternatively it could have been approached by people coming up from the south of Jura, where there is ample evidence of early habitation.

The importance of symbolism in the pre-literate world has already been considered and the use of the spiral motif in sacred locales since the Stone Age is irrefutable. Nowadays we are beginning to understand that contact between peoples was taking place over wider areas and on larger scale than has been previously realised. Partially this has been due to on over-reliance on the written word to understand the past. The old cliché of history being written by the winners is never truer than in matters concerning religion and belief.

However even the written word developed in societies where story telling was long established. Literacy is only a few thousand years old while most sensible people realise that humans have been on the planet for hundreds of thousands of years, and were not too different from us for much of that period. In Europe one of the earliest great pieces of literature, now understood to have been based on earlier oral traditions has recently been re-interpreted. *The Odyssey*, the journey of the Greek hero Odysseus, or Ulysses, after the Trojan Wars was written by Homer in the 8th century BCE. In his recent book *Odysseus and the Sea People*, Edo Nyland puts forward the claim that Odysseus's journey wasn't in the Mediterranean but in the Hebrides. He claims that the whirlpool Charybdis was originally The Corryvreckan and claims that Homer effectively 'masculinised' the story. Given what we know of cultural contacts long before Homer's time this is not impossible. If he is correct then this would reinforce the importance of The Corryvreckan as an early sacred site.

I hope that I have shown that The Corryvreckan is a good candidate for the deepest ideas behind the concept of the Holy Grail as it has developed over the centuries, and if I am right, millennia. The suggestion that we can understand something of the religious ides of the far past by an analysis of the landscape does I hope hold water. Just as Schliemann used Homer's Iliad to find the original location, we too can perhaps learn more by a judicious and careful look at the traditional tales that have survived in

Scotland. Where such tales of giants, particularly female, are linked to locales in the landscape with significant names, or which are the sites of ancient monuments. I think it perfectly acceptable to see such clusters of different types of evidence as proving that such places did have significance. The survival of such place names, like the telling of traditional tales reflects, even in the modern world, a continuity with the far past. Recurring motifs like the association of giant female figures with our highest mountains shows that these figures held a secure place in the shared imagination of our ancestors. The role of these females in creating the landscape, and being in control of the weather, emphasises that they were at one time Goddesses, or aspects of the one Mother Goddess. We have seen that it is likely the Christian monks who wrote of pagan beliefs organised the material along classically-influenced lines and thereby diminished the importance of female figures. The fact that so many different referents can be seen in the landscape tells us how important these female figures were. I have suggested an underlying duality, that of the Cailleach and Bride, which in itself reflects other dualities, Summer and Winter, day and night, hot and cold, life and death. So much evidence for this type of duality in the landscape suggests that the religious understanding behind it was very widespread if not universal. The continuities of usage of standing stones from at least the Bronze Age to the 1st Millennium is perhaps also reflected in some of the Pictish Symbols themselves. The symbol of the cauldron that crops up in votive offerings and on Symbol Stones is echoed by the ideas of the life-giving cauldrons in early texts and the cauldron is a symbol for life itself.

The idea that early peoples had an understanding of the world that was based around the idea of Mother Goddess has long been suggested. It is something that was most likely rooted in observation. The idea of male gods is not that old and the concept of a single male god only arrived in Britain less than twenty centuries ago. Before that there was the Mother Goddess. Although we can never be sure exactly what the Old Religion was, we can make several informed guesses. Further research is required into the existence of the Cailleach/Bride and the Carlin/Maiden polarities in the landscape but I hope that I have shown that there is a trail to be followed. The suggestion that significant hill-top locations became the sites of legends, names, rituals and ancient monuments is another area that should be looked at further. Many of the mounds scattered around Scotland have been interpreted as Mottes, part of specific Norman defensive structure. I have noted that too much has been made of the Roman presence in Scotland, and suggest the same is true of the Norman incomers. Many of the French or Norman genealogies claimed by aristocratic families are due to nothing more than fashion and have no basis in reality. An investigation of the Mottes would I believe show them to be much older than the Early Middle Ages. How many of our early Christian sites were, or are, on similar mounds? And is this because of the stated Christian policy of taking over the pagan precincts? If this is so this would also account for the fact that so many Pictish Symbol Stones have been found at or near churches. I have gone further and suggested that at least some of these mounds were seen as local versions of sacred mountains and again investigation of these mounds might show evidence for this. As to the sacred mountains themselves there may well have been different levels of sanctity. Some of these mountains like Ben Nevis, Lochnagar and Schiehallion are dangerous places and are always more likely to have a symbolic rather than a ritual significance. Smaller more accessible peaks like Edinburgh, Stirling and Dumbarton have associations with supposed early Christian saints who are clearly based on pagan originals. These locales were not only accessible, they were the natural focus for communal activity for the surrounding people long before they developed as military strongholds. Much of this is necessarily speculative but I think it makes sense. As I noted many of the suggested Scottish locales for the battles of Arthur appear to be precisely such centres of pagan activity and the invading Romans also visited several.

Many of the locales herein suggested as having sacral, mythological and legendary significance are in sight of each other. From Arthur's Seat in Edinburgh's Holyrood Park, when the weather is clear, one can see the Paps of Lothian, The Paps of Fife, Ben Ledi, Ben Lomond, Ben Arthur and Schiehallion over sixty miles away. On clear days in winter one can also see part of the Lochnagar massif. All of these mountains have clusters of different markers that suggest sacrality. While there are a great many Arthurian locales their significance lies partly in that they are a link to older beliefs. And the oldest belief is that of the Cailleach herself, the mother of humanity. And if all of this evidence associating her with mountains and specifically with breast-shaped locations is true it must reflect a deep held belief. I suggest the landscape has in fact held on to the proof of such belief. In one sense the Cailleach can be understood as not only creating the landscape but she is the landscape. The modern idea of Gaia that sees the world as essentially one super-organism is one that would seem to fit with what we can make out of the Old Religion. And if it was considered that she placed the breast-shaped peaks of Scotland to be noticed then surely in the awesome whirlpool of The Corryvreckan she surpassed herself. It is impossible to be sure but the widespread use of the spiral motif from the Stone Age onwards had to begin somewhere. Perhaps it arose from The Corryvreckan. If it was already well-established when people began arriving on Scotland's West Coast thousands of years ago, the fact that such a sacred symbol could be seen perpetually recurring in the environment must have had considerable effect. Either way The Corryvreckan is to this day truly awesome, as the breath of the goddess under the waves continues to throw spiralling water into the Atlantic tide.

Modern archaeologists are reluctant to dig up ancient sites unless there is a compelling reason to do so. They also prefer to investigate sites where they know what questions they can ask of the material they find. This is why so many Pictish archaeological investigations to date have been at Christian sites. We know quite a lot about early Christianity so such sites can be interpreted with a certain amount of confidence. Until now this has hardly been true of pre-Christian sites. If there is any value in the suggestions I have made regarding the Goddess in the landscape and the central importance of The Corryvreckan both physically and symbolically then things might change. Perhaps we can take a fresh look at the sites of Early Christian churches to see how many were raised on minds. We might be able to re-interpret hilltop sites by concentrating on their ritual rather than military significance. It is also perhaps worth considering how much symbolic meaning can be seen in some of our place names. The Cailleach was a goddess and became in time the word for a nun. Throughout Scotland there are local tales that tell of nunneries where we know there were none. Could these be remnants from a time when there were female priestess groups? I suggest that this is very likely. If I am correct in my reading of the landscape, there is much more that can be found out, from story, analysis of place names, studying alignment and walking the landscape itself. The Holy Grail grew from truly ancient ideas to become a mystical object that signifies many things – fertility, enlightenment, religious understanding. At a time when we and our planet faces many dangers, perhaps we can find out more of how our far-off ancestors saw their world – and hopefully learn from them.

The idea of the Quest that is at the heat of the Holy Grail motif is one I understand for it seems that I have been on a quest – a quest to try and understand how society developed in my native land. I studied history at university and always considered myself a hard-headed rationalist. The journey I have taken to try and understand the past has led me into areas of thought I did not expect and it often seemed that information I came across was as a result of following a path unseen. At a time when humanity needs all the help it can get to rise above the desolation and destruction that the rampant pursuit of short term greed posing as liberal capitalism has brought us, perhaps we can learn from looking at the past and trying to better understand how our ancestors succeeded in living in a more harmonious way with their environment. The Goddess was not just creator of life and death, she was how our ancestors conceived of the very existence of the planet that we are part of. Perhaps we should be prepared to learn from them.

Notes

Chapter Two

1. Darrah, J., *Paganism in Arthurian Romance*, p. 216
2. Koch, J.T., *The Gododdin of Anueurin*, p. xivi
3. Ginzberg, C., *Estasies: Deciphering the Witches' Sabbath*, p. 236
4. McHardy, S.A., *School of the Moon*
5. Campbell, E., *Were the Scots Irish?*
6. McHardy, S.A., *The Quest for Arthur*
7. Koch, p. xlii
8. Skene, W.F., *Four Ancient Books of Wales*; and Glennie, J.S., *Arthurian Locations*
9. Snyder, C., *Exploring the world of KING ARTHUR*, p. 128

Chapter Three

10. Dio Cassio, LXXVII, 12, 1-4
11. McHardy, S.A., *The Quest for Arthur*
12. McHardy, S.A., *The Quest for Arthur*, p. 67
13. Mackenzie, D.A., *Scottish Folklore and Folk Life*, p. 106

Chapter Four

14. Jocelyn, *Life of Kentigern*, in *Two Celtic Saints: The Lives of Ninian and Kentigern*
15. McHardy, S.A., *The Quest for the Nine Maidens*

Chapter Five

16. Isaacs, J., *Australian Dreaming: 40,000 years of Aboriginal History*

[17] Jones, G. and Jones, T., eds., *The Mabinogion*, p. 24

[18] Spence, L., *The Magic Arts in Celtic Britain*, p. 163

[19] Rees, A. and Rees, B., *Celtic Heritage*, p. 313

[20] Markdale, J., *Women of the Celts*, p. 105

[21] Swire, O., *The Highlands and Their Legends*, p. 48

[22] www.clannarthur.com

[23] Bede, *A History of the English Church and People*. trans. by L. Shirley-Price

Chapter Six

[24] Darrah, J., *Paganism in Arthurian Romance*, p. 228

[25] Mackenzie, D.A., *Scottish Folk-Lore and Folk Life*

[26] Campbell op cit

[27] Oram, R., *Scottish Prehistory*, p. 24

[28] Oram, R., *Scottish Prehistory*, p. 67

Chapter Seven

[29] Hope, A.D., *A Midsummer Eve's Dream*

[30] Barrow, G.W.S., *Religion in Scotland on the Eve of Christianity*

[31] Nicolaisen, W., *Scottish Place Names*, p. 169

[32] Drummond, P., *Scottish Mountain and Hill Names*, p. 90

[33] McHardy, S.A., *The Quest for the Nine Maidens*

Chapter Eight

[34] Mackenzie, W.C., *Scottish Place Names*

[35] Scott, D., *Watchers of the Dawn* CD

[36] Isaacs, J., *Australian Dreaming: 40,000 years of Aboriginal History*

[37] Wooing of Emer, www.ucc.ie.celt/online/T301021/

[38] Mackinlay, J.F., *The Deer Goddess Cult*
[39] Scrope, W., *Days of Deer-Stalking*, pp. 198-9

Chapter Nine

[40] McNeill, M., *The Silver Bough*, Vol. II, p. 20
[41] Davidson, H.R.E., *Lost Beliefs of Northern Europe*, p. 108
[42] Camus nam bearnach www.rcahms.gov.uk
[43] Hansen, W.F., *Saxo Grammaticus and Life of Hamlet*, p. 129
[44] Mackenzie, D.A., *Teutonic Myth and Legend*, p. 4f
[45] de Santillana, G., and von Dechend, H.,
[46] Gimbutas, M., *The Goddesses and Gods of Ancient Europe*

Bibliography

Allen, J. Romilly and Anderson, J., *The Early Christian Monuments of Scotland* (Balgavies, Angus: Pinkfoot Press, 1903)

Barrow, G.W.S., *Religion in Scotland on the eve of Christianity*, in P. Herde, *Gesammelte Abhandlungen and Aufsatze* (Stuttgart: Anton Hiersemann, 1997)

Bede, *A History of the English Church and People*, trans. by L. Sherley-Price, (London: Penguin Classics, 1955)

Chrétien de Troyes, *Arthurian Romances*, trans. by D.D.R. Own (London: Everyman's Library, 1987)

Campbell, E., *Were the Scots Irish?*, in *Antiquity* vol 75 (2001) pp. 285-292

Campbell, J.G., *Popular Tales of the West Highlands* (Edinburgh: Birlinn, repr. 1994)

Campbell, J., *The Hero with a Thousand Faces* (London: Abacus, 1975)

Darrah, J., *Paganism in Arthurian Romance* (Woodbridge: Boydell, 1994)

Davidson, H.R.E., *The Lost Beliefs of Northern Europe* (London: Routledge, 1993)

De Santillana, G. and von Dechend, H., *Hamlet's Mill* (London: Macmillan, 1970)

Dio Cassio in Millar, F., *A Study of Cassius Dio* (London: Oxford, 1964)

Drummond, P. *Scottish Mountain and Hill Names* (Glasgow: SMT, 1991)

Geoffrey of Monmouth, *The History of the Kings of Britain*, trans. by L. Thorpe (New York: Penguin, 1966)

Ginzburg, C., *Ecstasies: Deciphering the Witches' Sabbath* (New York: Pantheon Books, 1991)

Glennie, J.S., *Arthurian Localities* (Lampeter: Llanerch, repr., 1994)

Hansen, W.F., *Saxo Grammaticus and the Life of Hamlet* (Lincoln: University of Nebraska Press, 1993)

Hope, A.D., *A Midsummer's Eve's Dream* (Edinburgh: Oliver & Boyd, 1971)

Isaacs, J., *Australian Dreaming: 40,000 years of Aboriginal History* (Willoughby: Lansdowne Press, 1991)

James, S., *The Atlantic Celts* (London: British Museum Press, 1999)

Jocelyn, *Life of Kentigern*, in *Two Celtic Saints: The Lives of Ninian and Kentigern* (Lampeter: Llanerch, 1989)

Jones G. and Jones, T., eds., *The Mabinogion* (London: Everyman, 1993)

Koch, J.T., *The Gododdin of Aneurin* (Cardiff: University of Wales Press, 1997)

Mackay, J.G., *The Deer Goddess and Deer Goddess Cult in Scotland*, in *Folklore* vol 51 (1954)

Mackenzie, D.A., *Scottish Folk-Lore and Folk Life* (London: Blackie & Son, 1935)

Mackenzie, D.A., *Teutonic Myth and Legend* (London: Gresham, 1912)

MacKenzie, W.C., *Scottish Place Names* (London: Kegan Paul, 1931)

Mackinlay, J.F., *Traces of the Cultus of the Nine Maidens* in *Proceedings of the Society of Antiquaries of Scotland*, vol 1910

Malory, Thomas, *Le Morte D'Arthur*, ed. by J. Cowen (New York: Penguin, 1969)

Markale, J., *Women of the Celts* (Rochester: Inner Traditions International, 1986)

McHardy, S.A., *The Quest for Arthur* (Edinburgh: Luath, 2002)

McHardy, S.A., *The Quest for the Nine Maidens* (Edinburgh: Luath, 2004)

McHardy, S.A., *School of the Moon* (Edinburgh: Birlinn, 2004)

McNeill, M., *The Silver Bough*, 4 vols (Glasgow: Wm MacLellan, 1953-61)

Nennius *British History and the Welsh Annals*, ed. and trans. by J. Morris (London: Phillmore, 1980)

Nicolaisen, W.F.H., *Scottish Place-Names: Their Study & Significance* (Edinburgh: John Donald, 2001)

Oram, R., *Scottish Prehistory* (Edinburgh: Birlinn, 1997)

Oxbrow, M. and Robertson, I., *Rosslyn and the Grail* (Edinburgh: Mainstream, 2005)

Rees, A. and Rees, B., *Celtic Heritage* (London: Thames & Hudson, repr., 1990)

Rennie, J.A., *The Scottish People* (London: Hutchinson, 1960)

Scott, D., *Watchers of the Dawn* CD www.tain.org.uk/tain-silver-g.asp

Scrope, W., *Days of Deer-Stalking* (Glasgow: Hamilton, Adams & Co, 1883)

Sir Gawain and the Green Knight, trans. by B. Stone (New York: Penguin, 1979)

Sjoestedt, M.L., *Gods and Heroes of the Celts* (Blackrock: Four Courts Press, 1994)

Skene, W.F., *Four Ancient Books of Wales* www.sacred-texts.com/neu/celt/fab/index.htm

Snyder, C., *Exploring the World of KING ARTHUR* (London: Thames & Hudson, 2000)

Spence, L., *The Magic arts in Celtic Britain* (London: Constable, repr., 1995)

Swire, O., *The Highland and Their Legends* (Edinburgh: Oliver & Boyd, 1963)

The Quest of the Holy Grail, trans. by P.M. Matarasso (New York: Penguin, 1969)

Wace and Layamon, *The Life of King Arthur*, trans. by J. Weiss and R. Allen (London: Everyman's Library, 1997)

Wooing of Emer www.ucc.ie/celt/online/T301021

Index

Some other books published by **LUATH** PRESS

The Quest for the Nine Maidens
Stuart McHardy
ISBN 0 946487 66 9 £16.99

When King Arthur was conveyed to Avalon they were there. When Odin summoned warriors to Valhalla they were there. When Apollo was worshipped on Greek mountains they were there.
When Brendan came to the Island of Women they were there.

They tended the Welsh goddess Cerridwen's cauldron on inspiration, and armed the hero Peredur. They are found in Britain, Ireland, Norway, Iceland, Gaul, Greece, Africa and as far afield as South America and Oceania. They are the Nine Maidens – the priestesses of the Mother Goddess.

From the Stone Age to the twenty-first century, the Nine Maidens come in many forms – Muses, Maenads, Valkyries, seeresses and druidesses. In this book Stuart McHardy traces the Nine Maidens from both Christian and pagan sources, and begins to uncover one of the most ancient and widespread of human institutions.

The Quest for Arthur
Stuart McHardy
ISBN 1 84282 012 5 £16.99

King Arthur of Camelot and the Knights of the Round Table are enduring romantic figures. A national hero for the Bretons, the Welsh and the English alike, Arthur is a potent figure for many. This quest leads to a radical new knowledge of the ancient myth.

Historian, storyteller and folklorist Stuart McHardy believes he has uncovered the origins of this inspirational figure, the true Arthur. He incorporates knowledge of folklore and place-name studies with an archaeological understanding of the sixth century.

Combining knowledge of the earliest records and histories of Arthur with an awareness of the importance of oral traditions, this quest leads to the discovery that the enigmatic origins of Arthur lie not in Brittany, England or Wales. Instead they lie in that magic land the ancient Welsh called Y Gogledd, 'The North'; the North of Britain, which we now call – Scotland.

On the Trail of Scotland's Myths and Legends

Stuart McHardy

ISBN 1 84282 049 4 £7.99

Scotland is an ancient land with an extensive heritage of myths and legends that have been passed down by word-of-mouth over the centuries. As the art of storytelling bursts into new flower, many of these tales are being told again as they once were. As *On the Trail of Scotland's Myths and Legends* unfolds, mythical animals, supernatural beings, heroes, giants and goddesses come alive and walk Scotland's rich landscape as they did in the time of the Scots, Gaelic and Norse speakers of the past.

Visiting over 170 sites across Scotland Stuart McHardy traces the lore of our ancestors, connecting ancient beliefs with traditions still alive today. Presenting a new picture of who the Scottish are and where they have come from these stories provide an insight into a unique tradition of myth, legend and folklore that has marked the language and landscape of Scotland.

... a remarkably keen collection of tales.

NEIL MACARA BROWN, Scottish Book Collector

[Stuart McHardy is] passionate about the place of indigenous culture in Scottish national life.

COURIER AND ADVERTISER

Tales of the Picts

Stuart McHardy

ISBN 1 84282 097 4 £5.99

For many centuries the people of Scotland have told stories of their ancestors, a mysterious tribe called the Picts. This ancient Celtic-speaking people, who fought off the might of the Roman Empire, are perhaps best known for their Symbol Stones – images carved into standing stones left scattered across Scotland, many of which have their own stories. Here for the first time these tales are gathered together with folk memories of bloody battles, chronicles of warriors and priestesses, saints and supernatural beings. From Shetland to the Border with England, these ancient memories of Scotland's original inhabitants have flourished since the nation's earliest days and now are told afresh, shedding new light on our ancient past.

The Quest for the Celtic Key

Karen Ralls-MacLeod and Ian Robertson
ISBN 1 84282 084 2 £7.99

Full of mystery, magic and intrigue, Scotland's past is still burning with unanswered questions. Many of these have been asked before, some have never before been broached – but all are addressed with the inquisitiveness of true detectives in The Quest for the Celtic Key. This is a collaboration between medieval Celtic historian Karen Ralls-MacLeod and Scottish Masonic researcher Ian Robertson, both of whom explore and unearth with relish the little known facts embedded within early Scottish history.

Who was the 'Wizard of the North'?

Was Winston Churchill really a practising member of a Druid order?

What are the similarities between Merlin and Christ?

Did Arthur, king of the Britons, conquer Scotland and was he buried in Govan?

Were the 3,500 year-old tartan-wearing mummies in China's Takla Makan desert Scottish?

What is hidden in the vaults at Rosslyn Chapel?

Why is the lore surrounding Scottish freemasonry so unique?

Encompassing well-known events and personae – such as Robert the Bruce, William Wallace, the Declaration of Arbroath and the Stone of Destiny – whilst also tackling the more obscure elements in Scottish history – the significance of the number 19, the power of the colour green and the spiritual meaning of locations across Scotland – The Quest for the Celtic Key illustrates how the seemingly disparate 'mysteries of history' are connected.

A travelogue which enriches the mythologies and histories so beautifully told, with many newly wrought connection to places, buildings stones and other remains.

REV. DR MICHAEL NORTHCOTT, Faculty of Divinity, University of Edinburgh

Luath Press Limited
committed to publishing well written books worth reading

LUATH PRESS takes its name from Robert Burns, whose little collie Luath (*Gael.*, swift or nimble) tripped up Jean Armour at a wedding and gave him the chance to speak to the woman who was to be his wife and the abiding love of his life. Burns called one of *The Twa Dogs* Luath after Cuchullin's hunting dog in *Ossian's Fingal*. Luath Press was established in 1981 in the heart of Burns country, and is now based a few steps up the road from Burns' first lodgings on Edinburgh's Royal Mile.

Luath offers you distinctive writing with a hint of unexpected pleasures.

Most bookshops in the UK, the US, Canada, Australia, New Zealand and parts of Europe either carry our books in stock or can order them for you. To order direct from us, please send a £sterling cheque, postal order, international money order or your credit card details (number, address of cardholder and expiry date) to us at the address below. Please add post and packing as follows: UK – £1.00 per delivery address; overseas surface mail – £2.50 per delivery address; overseas airmail – £3.50 for the first book to each delivery address, plus £1.00 for each additional book by airmail to the same address. If your order is a gift, we will happily enclose your card or message at no extra charge.

Luath Press Limited
543/2 Castlehill
The Royal Mile
Edinburgh EH1 2ND
Scotland

Telephone: 0131 225 4326 (24 hours)
Fax: 0131 225 4324
email: sales@luath.co.uk
Website: www.luath.co.uk